50 SHADES OF SALES

UNLOCK THE HANDCUFFS OF FEAR AND IGNORANCE TO
STOKE MASSIVE GROWTH AT YOUR CPA FIRM!

PATRICK MALAYTER, CPA, FOUNDER
CPA GROWTH PARTNERS

Published & distributed by:
Patrick Malayter

in association with:
IBJ Book Publishing
41 E. Washington St., Suite 200
Indianapolis, IN 46204
www.ibjbp.com

Library of Congress Control Number: 2015937001
ISBN 978-1-939550-18-7
First Edition
Printed in the United States of America

DEDICATION PAGE

I dedicate this book to . . .

Ellen, the love of my life!

Our children Megan, Leslie, Keely, James and Jacqueline—for they have each given me an enormous sense of purpose.

My fellow partners and colleagues in the accounting profession at KPMG, LLP, Olive, LLP, and BKD, LLP—especially Dave Stafseth who helped me develop so many skills and Rick Taylor who opened my eyes to an entirely new world.

I am an incredibly blessed person to have had all of you in my life!

Patrick Malayter

ACKNOWLEDGEMENTS

The author would like to thank the following individuals contributing to this book:

Ellen Malayter for her ongoing counsel and editorial assistance.

Jacqueline "Jacki" Malayter for assistance in crafting the book's illustrations.

Holly Weaver for editorial-related work.

The staff at 99designs.com for their work on crowdsourcing the book's cover, in particular Alexander Vulcheff, the winning designer.

The professionals at IBJ Book Publishing in Indianapolis, Indiana—especially Pat Keiffner and Jodi Belcher.

CONTENTS

BUT, I DIDN'T STUDY ACCOUNTING TO BE IN SALES

Yes, I *know*, you didn't study accounting to be in sales . . . *neither* did I. My guess is that your attorney buddy didn't attend law school to be in sales. Nor did your high school classmates that opted for trade school versus college to become plumbers and electricians intend to be salesmen, although a chunk of their day is likely dedicated to selling, *especially* if they have their own shop. Probably most of your firm's business and nonprofit clientele likewise weren't chomping at the bit to become sales people when they started their organizations or entered their vocation, yet *many* are. The fact is, if you are passionate about being an owner or in leadership at most enterprises, *especially today's CPA firms*, being skilled at influence, persuasion, and sales are key attributes. Fortunately for you, these are learnable skills, pretty much like everything else you've mastered at your firm.

For many in the CPA business, the term "sales" carries a somewhat greasy connotation. Perhaps you think if you do great work and your firm has a fine reputation, clients will just flock-in. In today's world, that's wrong-way thinking. Many other thought-industry-professionals make that same error in judgment. Peter Thiel, for example, a partner at Founders Fund, a Silicon Valley venture capital fund, and a co-founder of billion-dollar companies PayPal and Palantir Technologies, notes in his book *Zero to One* that engineering-types (he calls them "the nerds"), view the superiority of their know-how as being the main driver of company sales, placing low value on the sales function.[i] Thiel's VC experience gives him a totally different perspective, because he's seen multiple companies sink, not because of poor products or services, but because of lousy sales skills.[ii] Thiel also observes that the more important the sale is to a customer, in terms of money or risk, the more likely the prospect wants to meet with other key members of the provider's management team, in addition to the engagement professionals.[iii] Based on Thiel's outlook, CPA firm managing partners, industry niche leaders, and perhaps others up the food chain, need to embrace these ideas too.

Two obvious, but very important assumptions are implicit in this book:

1. Your firm and you are already *great* at your craft, and not in the habit of over-promising and under-delivering. Just as you can't build a house without laying a stable foundation first—placing robust sales-related techniques to drive new clients, and additional fees from existing clients, will implode on your firm where you can't deliver effectively.

2. Most CPAs are honest as the day is long. Some of the technologies discussed herein can be used manipulatively, even though we are teaching them to be employed constructively. I assume your periodic ethics classes have rubbed-off on you, and that you generally believe that bad karma strikes people that do bad things.

Surely there is a reason you're reading these words now. Perhaps you're a manager or senior manager at your firm, and you know to make partner you must demonstrate business development skills or create a practice for yourself, but no one at your shop has provided you tools or comprehensive training. Maybe you're already a partner, and you're being pressed by management to somehow grow your book in today's still-tough economy to replace lost work, or you're facing a downward comp adjustment. Possibly, you lead an office, industry team or have been tapped by your firm to head-up a new initiative, and are striving for ways to stoke top-line revenue. Or, you're the CEO of a Top 100 Firm, and your shop has been languishing in the bottom quartiles of annual CPA firm growth rankings for years, with your firm becoming less and less relevant, and subject to greater earnings pressure.

As President Clinton said, "I feel your pain." More than just feel your pain though, I *passionately* believe there are proven ways to radically change your situation—for the good, using practical, learnable methods and approaches, which are highlighted and taught in this book.

If you've ever searched Amazon for books or videos about CPA sales and marketing training, or Googled to find dedicated CPA firm sales training from those who have *actually built or grown substantial practices within a CPA firm environment—engaging in real accounting services prospect-sales sessions*, you'll find fairly limited results. Actually you'll find none, until now that is.

That dearth of resources isn't a new thing. As a younger professional at KPMG, then Peat Marwick Mitchell & Co., I cobbled together my extra cash to buy sales-related books, *none* of which applied to professional services, and *all* of which advocated using cheesy, heavy-handed techniques. KPMG's internal sales training back then (which I never actually participated in) was rooted in a Xerox-based methodology, and attendees I spoke with came back more confused about selling after their CPE session, presumably because the firm didn't sell copiers. My office had no real rainmakers to emulate, although there were many truly *outstanding* client service professionals. Consequently, I spent most of my business development time selling additional services to existing clientele, and became masterful at it. That was a sufficient level of business-development acumen for me to make partner at KPMG at the time.

When KPMG divested certain non-strategic offices, I landed at Olive, LLP, and became the Firm's National Tax Director shortly after. Our CEO, John Harris, directed me towards creating various service lines and practices. Building practices from scratch requires a multitude of talents, and sales and marketing are at the top. With the scarcity of top-shelf resources for professional services sales training, I went on a multi-year journey of study to craft a unique approach that would thrive in a CPA or advisory firm setting. My journey included obtaining Practitioner and Master Practitioner Certifications in neuro-linguistic programing[iv] (NLP), a communications-based psychology subfield, completing hypnosis certification training to better understand influential language patterns, participating in multiple high-level Robbins Research International Inc. trainings, studying at university-sponsored business strategy courses, and reading hundreds of books on human motivation, psychology, sales, business strategy, language patterns, innovation, marketing, and advertising writing.

The above-noted educational expedition culminated in two accountant-focused CPE-related classes on goal setting and achievement, *Seizing the Reins of Change*, and persuasion in accounting services selling and business settings, *Unstoppable Influence*. Such learnings were also vital in my founding or contributing significantly to the development of six specialty consulting and tax practices which generated multi-million dollar revenues and profits—as well as being instrumental in designing several growth-inducing tax initiatives during my years as National Tax Director at Olive, LLP, and later, BKD, LLP.

As you know, knowledge is *only* powerful when applied. Take action, and make a difference for your firm and yourself with the tools you'll learn herein!

Patrick M. Malayter, CPA, Founder

CPA Growth Partners

Preface References

[i] Thiel, Peter. *Zero to One*. New York: Crown Books, 2014. Page 127

[ii] Ibid. Page 130

[iii] Ibid. Page 132

[iv] Neuro-linguistic programing was co-developed/created by Richard Bandler (an author and trainer in the field of self-help) and John Grinder (a linguist, author, management consultant, trainer and speaker) in 1975.

CHAPTER 1

YOUR MINDSET . . .

Your mindset, it's a pretty broad subject area. There are many in the field of human motivation that would say, success in any activity is 90% psychology or mindset, 10% mechanics. I don't know if those percentages are true or not. The characteristics and quality of one's psychology, is fairly difficult to measure precisely. I **do** know with strong certainty, to the extent you have a poor psychology, your chances for failure in most any undertaking are pretty much 100%. **For that reason, this is probably one of the most important sections of the book!**

In this chapter we will explore a number of topics that accountants normally don't examine—areas such as "the power of why," beliefs and the fears of failure and rejection. However, before delving into that, it's helpful to prod you by reviewing a bit about the state of the accounting industry, and how . . .

The Rich Will Get Richer . . . and the Poor Poorer

Studying the *Accounting Today* Top 100 Firms' growth patterns for the past several years is rather telling. Adjusting for factors like major mergers—such as the CliftonLarsonAllen, Dixon Hughes Goodman and CohnResnick fusions and the Plante Moran/Blackman Kallick combination; "top-quartile growers" expanded at an average and median rate of 14.3% and 13.4% for the past 3-year span; whereas "bottom quartile growth firms" approximated .6% and 1.5% during such timeframe, respectively.[i] One great aspect of you being a CPA, is that you understand basic financial principles like the "Rule of 72"—and thus, how these bottom quartile firms are "speeding down the highway of irrelevance" during the next five years, compared to peers in the top quartile, should these growth trends continue.

As you know, subnormal growth creates lots of other headaches—besides just irrelevance, including:

- An inability to add net new partners,

- The loss of high-potential staff,

- Net-income-per-partner pressures,

- Impeding the desire and/or ability to invest in new services or markets,

- Creating constraints on funding retirement-related payouts, and

- Causing roadblocks to remain an independent firm.

In short, it can bring about a death spiral for your firm. Certainly, the foregoing data highlights how select firms, and their professionals, will need to generate growth in the future. Otherwise, as the subtitle implies—they will likely get a *lot* poorer.

The Power of "Why"

Anytime you are embarking on a new goal or are learning a new subject area, such as mastering influence, persuasion and sales skills, it's imperative to know your why. Having a strong *why* can often provide you with the rocket fuel boost that sends you on your way.

For me, a memorable event illustrating the power of why involved an encounter with a life insurance salesman. In the summer of 1986, an insurance agent from one of the big shops visited me at our office in an attempt to sell his wares. During the conversation, he learned that my wife and I had three girls under the age of five. Trying to impress me on the need to save, and how whole life insurance would be such a wonderful tool to do that, he emphasized that it would take nearly $200,000 for my wife/I to send these three little girls to a state college (double that for private universities). And, of course, I'd have those three daughters to marry off someday. At the time, I was earning somewhere between $40,000 and $45,000. That $200,000 sum was such an extraordinary amount of money, the insurance salesman might as well have said college and weddings would cost me $200 billion! Talk about getting hit upside the head with a 2x4—I can still feel the cold sweat I broke into at the moment. Although the agent didn't make a sale that day, I knew then I better find a way to make partner. There were tons of *whys* for making partner besides the many forthcoming financial obligations, but achieving that overall goal would require developing sales/business development talents (along with improving many other skills).

As the years passed and I was involved in creating practices, the whys took on a whole new dimension and were largely other-focused. For example, during the inevitable ups and downs in building these practice units, the whys to succeed included:

- Having an obligation to employees and their families who were depending on the success of the business to provide their living.

- Responsibility to my fellow partners who were entrusting me with the firm's capital to build a practice.

- Our firm needing the services to distinguish ourselves in the marketplace.

- Personal pride: like most in the CPA business, I wanted to do an excellent job.

How about you? What are your particular whys to master the influence, persuasion and sales techniques being taught in this book? As Mick Jagger sings on the Rolling Stones' 1969 album *Let it Bleed*, "You Can't Always Get What You Want . . . **You Get What You Need!**"

So why is getting *great* at this book's material a must for you? Take ten minutes now, dig deep, and list out five to ten "whys" detailing your commitment to mastering this material—it's okay to get emotional about it:

_____

_____

_____

_____

_____

_____

_____

The power of why doesn't just apply to individuals—firms, functional units (e.g., your audit, tax or consulting practice), industry teams and offices need to figure out their "whys" as well. Any firm or the aforementioned teams struggling with growth would probably find it useful in a partner/manager meeting to openly discuss **why** significantly improving its organic revenue expansion is an absolute "must" for them. Reasons obviously vary, however they might include in part:

- Creating rewarding career opportunities for the staff.

- Improving net income per partner.

- Ensuring the continuity and future of the firm.

- Building a solid industry-focused client base.

- Bolstering the firm's reputation in the marketplace.

- It's flat-out fun when we are growing.

- Etc.

Okay leaders: It's time for you to list out all your whys detailing your commitment to mastering this material as a team—and ramping-up your unit's top-line performance by several additional digits of growth (You'll probably need a lot more pages to write on.):

_____

_____

_____

_____

_____

_____

_____

_____

_____

_____

_____

_____

Many high-achievers really emphasize this power of why, noting that reasons for success come first, with the answers and actions following. If your reasons aren't robust enough to get your motor running, go back and tighten them up.

This leads us to our next important mindset factor:

Beliefs . . . Whether You Think You Can or Can't, You're Right

As noted, becoming capable in domains of influence, persuasion and sales are truly valuable for both for your firm and you. So a natural question is, "What is a roadblock that can stop you from even starting?"

The short answer is, "your BS," or, more specifically, your limiting Belief Systems.

Your beliefs. We're not talking religion here, we're talking psychology. Essentially, what you believe to be true has a *profound* impact on what you're willing to do, and how intensely you're willing to pursue it. In my lengthy CPA career, I've heard (and occasionally, held) a bunch of limiting beliefs. My guess is that you've heard some of the limiting BS, such as:

- We've never done that before (so don't ask us to try now).

- Our partner group isn't capable of _____(selling, learning how to do _____).

- We can't compete with _____ (pick your competitor).

- We haven't ever created a _____ practice, so it's unlikely we'll do it now.

- We're too busy to _____ (reach out to CPA Growth Partners for help, etc.).

The BS list can go on and on and on—leaving your firm and you "stuck."

Of course, bosses, colleagues, and family can have a huge impact on the beliefs you adopt. Accordingly, you should be cognizant of the comments you make to others when they come to you with an idea. Likewise, it's important for you to stand guard at the door of your mind when someone advises you that an idea you hold is impossible.

This happened to me in the late 1990s. In 1997, I was tasked with starting an engineering-based cost segregation practice. I hired as our technical leader Price Waterhouse's National Director of that service line. Our firm at the time, Olive, LLP, was about the seventeenth largest CPA firm in the U.S. and did not have the clientele to support such a high-powered professional, even though we had a dedicated sales professional to sell services outside our client base. One of the books I was reading at the time, *Money Making Secrets of Marketing Genius Jay Abraham and Other Marketing Wizards*—written by Mr. Abraham, discussed a concept called host devices, a marketing concept similar to what we would call "affiliate marketing" today.[ii]

Using the host devices notion, I perceived we could form alliances with other CPA firms throughout the U.S. that did not have the resources to hire such an expensive/capable professional, where our firm could perform engineering-based studies for them on a fee-sharing arrangement. By having such alliances, we could normalize the stream of projects for our cost segregation team by having each of the CPA firm clients sell projects to their clientele. Further, it would ultimately reduce our selling costs related to travel and so on. I was pretty fired-up about my breakthrough idea, but when I enthusiastically explained it to my mentor over breakfast, he said it was, "One of the dumbest ideas he'd ever heard."

Fortunately, I stood guard at the door of my mind at the time, and didn't adopt his limiting beliefs with respect to the CPA alliance concept. Within a two-year period, such cost segregation practice was generating more than three-million dollars of net revenue, with a 45-percent net profit. Roughly 70 percent of the fees were generated by the CPA alliance partners. The practice ultimately became one of the most dominant in the country, growing to 10 full-time engineers, and was featured in the *Journal of Accountancy*.

A seminal thinker in the area of beliefs is author, trainer, and technology developer Robert Dilts. In his 1990 book, *Changing Belief Systems with NLP*, Dilts highlights the relationship of one's identity, beliefs, perception of capabilities, and resulting behaviors as follows:[iii]

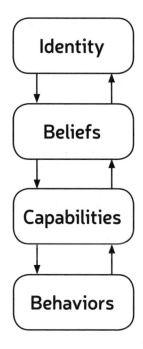

In Dilts' hierarchical model, how a person defines or "identifies themselves" directly impacts their personal beliefs and values. One's "beliefs and values" influences their views and perceptions of what their capabilities are. Further, a person's self-judgments about their "capabilities" can drive their behaviors in multiple contexts. As the model illustrates, Dilts notes the model's components are interactive, so specific social and developmental experiences (i.e., behaviors), could impact how a person views their capabilities— and thus, influence their beliefs and identity.[iv]

Here's an example of how Dilts' model might play out using certain commonly-held stereotypes about those in the accounting profession.[v] Let's assume you define yourself by what you do for a living, so you might say, "I'm a CPA (or an accountant, audit partner or tax professional)." Typecast beliefs or values about CPAs might include being less extraverted, content to be alone, more reserved, formal, skeptical and cautious (these stereotypes

may not belong to you).[vi] People holding such personal beliefs or values likely wouldn't think they have the capability to be stars at networking events or be able to comfortably handle cold calls to prospective clients. Consequently, if forced to attend a networking event cocktail party, they'll probably hangout with a buddy from the office, or stand in the corner, alone, nursing a beer—and they'll likely let those prospect cold calls slide continuously to the bottom of their work to-do list.

So, what do you do if you're unhappy about a belief you hold?

A simple first step to lessening the impact of your limiting beliefs is to become cognizant of them. Just becoming consciously aware of some of your self-imposed boundaries, for example, might cause you to stop and say to yourself, "That's nonsense—I don't believe that!"

Awareness helps, but generally isn't the silver bullet to ending a limiting belief's impact. There are multiple techniques that *can* work to help put a disempowering belief to bed though. Here's an exercise that will take about an hour that should help to weaken one of your limiting beliefs.

1. Write down your limiting belief.
   Example: *We'll never be able to convert a federal tax professional into a specialist in international taxation—it will be too expensive and no one has interest; it just won't ever work here.*

_____

_____

_____

_____

2. Write down at least twenty specific reasons that articulate how that limiting belief has cost you and your firm in the past and how it's doing so in the present.

   Example: *We have been losing key proposals on complex clients in the Miami market because we do not have that needed specialty in our practice unit.*

_____

_____

_____

_____

_____

_____

_____

_____

_____

_____

_____

_____

_____

11

3. Write out a list of at least twenty specific costs and other losses that your firm and/or you will feel in the future to the extent you continue holding onto this limiting belief.
Example: *Our two biggest clients will be at risk because the XYZ CPA Firm has this expertise in-house, and they'd absolutely love to steal them as clients.*

_____

_____

_____

_____

_____

_____

_____

_____

_____

_____

_____

_____

_____

4. Identify, and write out an empowering belief. This is (often) the antithesis of the limiting belief you noted above.
   Example: *We have some real stars in our tax department, who can be the international specialists we want, as long as we're totally committed to the outcome.*

   _____

   _____

   _____

5. On the same piece of paper, write out at least twenty-five specific benefits or wins your firm and you will achieve by embracing this new empowering belief.
   Example: *Our firm will be able to perform work on several of the high-profile manufacturers in South Florida with this new specialty—it really expands our market potential.*

   _____

   _____

   _____

   _____

   _____

   _____

   _____

   _____

_____

_____

_____

_____

_____

_____

_____

_____

_____

_____

_____

_____

You might not wipe out that limiting belief completely, but you're going to be far more open to options and possibilities, and give you way more resources.

This is just one of many techniques you can do individually, or use in group settings, that can put that BS in its grave.

Now, let's look at another area where many of us stop ourselves.

Destroying Fears That Cause You to Quit

Let's pretend your firm and you get past the limiting BS—would you like to know what two fears will likely cause you to quit, so you can plan for them in advance? Before we get started, here's a little background.

Would you agree that a huge number of CPA firm partners, and partner hopefuls, are more ambitious than the average person you'd meet on the street? You'd probably say yes.

Personal development life coach and self-help author Tony Robbins hypothesizes the "determination" many high-achievers in the business world possess, particularly businessmen, is principally rooted in significance, one of his categorized *Six-Human-Needs*[vii]. Significance is the need to be and feel important, to have meaning and consequence, to think one's life matters. The late behavioral psychologist Abraham Maslow might classify that drive as being grounded in the need for esteem. The lower version of esteem being the need for respect from others, including the need for status, recognition, fame, prestige, and attention; with the higher version being self-respect.

A couple moods, outlooks or emotional states that run directly counter to significance/esteem are the feelings of failure and rejection. Oftentimes, just the possibility of experiencing rejection is enough to shut a person down. This fear of failure and/or fear of rejection isn't necessarily always a bad thing. Having an appropriate fear of failure might stoke you into preparing more diligently for an upcoming meeting with the IRS, PCAOB or other regulators—or dissuade imprudent behaviors like emulating a dangerous stunt performed by a movie's action hero. Ditto with a healthy fear of rejection that keeps you from carelessly blurting out slurs.

15

The problem arises when these two fears become unfounded, unreasonable and/or incapacitating and preclude your teammates and you from taking some fairly normal and necessary actions, such as:

- Making cold calls to prospective clients to set up introductory appointments.

- Continuing to follow up to schedule meetings when your voicemail or e-mail messages aren't returned.

- Asking for an opportunity to issue a proposal and/or provide a complimentary service.

- Providing much-needed constructive feedback to a colleague or client.

- Introducing one of your firm's consulting-related services to an existing client.

- Executing action steps to initiate a new practice or service or improve an underperforming unit.

- Learning new soft skills, such as the material in this book.

- Valuing billing for a great result your team delivered.

- Requesting a referral from an important client.

- Seeking out opportunities to speak at prestigious events.

I'm sure you can think of a few other examples, too, things that tighten your gut just thinking of them.

So, if embracing a personally frightening fear of failure and fear of rejection is truly problematic, how can you overcome it? Although there are many methods, one of the more effective is used by Robbins in a multi-day event he calls *Date With Destiny*[viii], a life-changing seminar you should strongly consider attending. In part of the conference, attendees highlight negative emotional states they want to rid themselves of, such as an irrational fear of failure or rejection—and craft rules for when it is appropriate to feel those feelings. In short, the aim is to design rules making it hard to feel bad. The format for creating a new rule being:

"I would only have this feeling if I were to consistently believe _____, instead of realizing _____ _____.

So, for yours truly, my rules for excessive fears of failure and rejection were deconstructed using this process:

Consistent Destructive Fear of Failure: I would *only* have this feeling if I were to *consistently* focus on the *deceitful belief* that I could always fail, **instead** of recognizing that I've triumphed *anytime* I've either learned something through the process and/or I have given my all.

Consistent Debilitating Feelings of Rejection: I would *only* have this feeling if I were to *consistently* believe my worth or value as a person rests in the opinion of someone else, i.e., they can in fact reject me, **instead of** realizing I'm the *only* person who determines how I feel.

Having new rules for a debilitating fear of failure or rejection might be just hunky-dory, but they'll do absolutely nothing for you if you can't access them to blow-past discouragement or your wanting to quit as needed. So, how can you incorporate them into your behavior naturally?

Some of the better discussions or discoveries about inoculating oneself against fears, self-doubt and negative self-talk, including an extreme fear of failure, come from within the sports psychology arena. A key means for elite athletes to make constructive thought or emotional states more automatic in the face of difficult competition involves incantations and affirmations. In this context, affirmations and incantations are simply positive verbal statements that, as repeated over time, drive enhanced performance. In athletic domains, the goal is to integrate the affirmation and its feeling into one's life so that its message becomes part of the individual's makeup and beliefs. The approach isn't like flipping a light switch—it takes some time—but is deemed to have positive effects on athletes' thinking initially, followed by their mood and, ultimately, their performance.[ix]

Okay, I know you're probably not an elite athlete, but the aforementioned sports psychology affirmations and incantation approach might make sense as a way for you to inoculate yourself against irrational fears of failure and rejection in business settings. As noted above, it requires some diligence. Initially, you might need to spend 10 to 15 minutes a day for a couple of weeks, shouting your new affirmations aloud to get them ingrained. Further, you will want to print or write out these new rules in a large font and place them in a prominent place such as near your office phone or computer so you can refresh your memory of them in tough work-related situations.

If you're thinking to yourself, "Sounds like some pretty crazy stuff. Are you trying to make me look foolish in front of my co-workers— and have you actually used it?" The short answers are, no, I don't want you to feel uncomfortable in front of your co-workers, so you might want to do those affirmations at home—and, yes, I have personally done affirmations. I've found that creating rules for overcoming irrational fears of failure and rejection have been incredibly helpful while my teams and I initiated several highly-profitable practices from scratch. Dealing with these dual fears, enabled teammates and I to perform uncomfortable tasks like cold-calling and handling doubting colleagues through the incubation process. We also had a massive goal map on my office wall that included these failure/rejection rules, so we could reference and remind ourselves of them regularly.

I totally get it that some of you probably think this is too New Age to incorporate into your life. Nevertheless, many can get so locked-up by fear, that they're eager to explore new avenues. So, if that is your desire or ambition, I'd invite you to consider taking the actions noted herein. The only things you'll lose are your irrational, incapacitating fears.

Chapter 1 References

[i]*Accounting Today Magazine* is a publication of SourceMedia. *The Accounting Today* Top 100 constitutes intellectual property of *Accounting Today Magazine*. Recalculating the Top 100 rankings on a three-year basis (and adjusting for major mergers where published data was available) reflects an average per year growth rate, median per year growth amount, and average per year growth rate range of "bottom quartile firms" of .55 percent, 1.5 percent, and -6.45 percent to 3.42 percent, respectively. Similarly calculated three-year amounts for "top quartile firms" were 14.31 percent, 13.41 percent, and 11.11 percent to 19.31 percent, respectively. The three-year average per year growth rate for Big Four firms was 10.83 percent—implying healthy growth is possible notwithstanding a firm's substantial size. The three-year period ended with the 2014 data published by *Accounting Today Magazine*.

[ii]Abraham, Jay. *Money-Making Secrets of Marketing Genius Jay Abraham and Other Marketing Wizards*. Abraham Publishing Group, Rolling Hills Estates, CA, 1994. Page 31

[iii]Dilts, Robert. *Changing Belief Systems with NLP*. Meta Publications, Capitola, CA, 1990. Page 1

[iv]Ibid. Pages 1-10

[v]Coate, Charles J.; Mitschow, Mark C.; Schinski, Michael D. *What Students Think of CPAs: Is The Stereotype Alive and Well? The CPA Journal of NYSSCPA*. August, 2003. Note—during 2000, academics W. Steve Albrecht, Ph.D. and Robert J. Sack, CPA conducted a comprehensive study on business students' perceptions about

accountants and their personalities. The survey showed that those responding perceived accountants to be somewhat less extroverted than the average individual, more formal and reserved, content to be alone, and non–thrill-seeking. Interestingly, the results noted accountants were viewed as possessing greater leadership qualities. Further, in a characteristic facet known as the agreeable dimension, survey participant's perceived accountants to be less agreeable or likable than the average individual. Accountants were viewed as having a tendency to be skeptical, blunt, and somewhat competitive. The strongest and most pronounced perceived differences between accountants and the average individual were found in an area described as the "conscientiousness dimension of personality" . . . with accountants perceived to be very capable, ordered, principled, diligent, self-motivated, and cautious.

[vi]Ibid.

[vii]*Six-Human-Needs* technology represents intellectual property of the Anthony Robbins Companies.

[viii]*Date With Destiny* is a registered trademark and intellectual property of the Anthony Robbins Companies.

[ix]Kauss, David, PhD, *Mastering Your Inner Game*. Champaign, IL,: Human Kinetics, 2001. Pages 180-183

CHAPTER 2

PERSONAL SKILLS YOU'LL NEED TO MASTER

This section focuses on a number of learnable personal skills that you'll need to become highly effective at to achieve excellence in influence, persuasion and sales. Moreover, these are life skills, in that they will make you better in many interpersonal settings, such as recruiting, client meetings, discussions with your bosses and your home life. These lessons probably should have been part of our business-school education, but then, everyone would have these unfair abilities that you'll now singularly possess.

The skills we'll study include rapport, listening, effective question asking, magic words, basic language patterns, goal setting, and the power of grit. You might be thinking, "Wow, these are principles that I already know, so I'll save some time and just skip this chapter." In my years of observation, however, these are skills that many professionals—*especially* CPAs—truly struggle with, (and consequently limit their potential). So, do yourself a favor and pay attention.

Creating Compelling Rapport

The notion of rapport can most easily be summarized in one statement: when people are like each other, they tend to like each other. It's the fall of 2014 as I'm writing these words, so, for fun, let's look at the five countries of the world that are reported to *most* dislike the United States, and some of the similarities and differences between them and us. These countries currently have the most unfavorable view of the U.S., along with their economic circumstances and the relative strength of their negative views:[i]

Country	Per Capita GDP	Unfavorable View %
Iraq	$7,100	67%
Yemen	$2,300	69%
Lebanon	$15,800	71%
Pakistan	$3,100	73%
Palestinian Territory	N/A	80%

When you think about these countries, does the U.S. have similar economics and per capita prosperity? Do we speak the same language? Do we have substantially similar religious views, practices, and tolerances, operate in a like fashion governmentally, including judicial rights, and do we hold consistent values with respect to education, a woman's role in society, and other social mores? Mostly not, and although I haven't seen surveys of U.S. citizens' views on these particular countries, my sense is we wouldn't see strong favorability rankings towards them either. Now compare these countries to your general perceptions of sovereignties like Australia, Canada, Ireland, and England, and consider the differences?

Now, think about the conventions you regularly attend, such as AICPA sessions, state society events, or meetings within your firm's industry teams. As you think about these gatherings, you'll probably recall that there was an instant bond among the attendees, even in situations where you've never met some of those people before. At many of the ACG Capital Connections that

I attended during my private equity days, there was immediate rapport among the conventioneers because they were either looking for a deal, working on a deal, seeking to get financing for deals, or attempting to become a service provider to a deal. Everything was deal-centric.

Consider your activities outside of work for a moment. Are you part of a club where all the members have disparate interests? Probably not. Your organization is likely formed around some common interest like ownership of Corvettes, your affiliation or support of a specific college, or passion for a local sports team.

When you think about those you hold in high esteem, and evaluate what makes them so appealing, in all likelihood it involves the ways in which they are similar to you, or at a minimum, the way you aspire to be. You're probably *not* thinking, "Even though we differ in almost every conceivable way—politically, socially, leisure interests, activities, and values—I want to hang out with them all the time!" When you think of those likeable people, you probably say to yourself, "They see the world in much the same way I do." In their book, *NLP—The New Technology of Achievement*, the NLP Comprehensive Training Team notes that research demonstrates that more than 80 percent of all sales are based on the customer liking the sales professional. The same study shows that people are more apt to stay in jobs where they feel liked and appreciated, versus work where they might even be paid more money. No doubt, your attention to building rapport can have a huge impact on areas, including:

- Setting calls with prospects

- Influencing decision-makers

- Attracting new business

• Selling additional services to existing customers

• Retaining existing business

• Persuading others[ii]

A number of old school sales training approaches suggest the way to create rapport is to match life experiences or other interests of that person. That might be okay as an initial icebreaker, but can be inauthentic and comical to the extent it carries on for any length of time. For example, many years ago, a colleague of mine and I were making a prospect call to an ag-bank in the Midwest. Our main contact had an unusual interest in, and hobby involving antique farm equipment. My teammate, who did not grow up on a farm or have any other agricultural background, feigned deep interest for and knowledge of this topic, with conversation continuing for twenty minutes or more. In addition to eating away at our valuable appointment time, my colleague's fascination was contrived and ultimately uncomfortable. We didn't walk away with any new work that day, either.

So, what's an alternative? In a landmark study, psychologist Albert Mehrabian, determined the following:

• Only 7 percent of what is communicated between individuals is through words themselves.

• 38 percent is rooted in vocal expression, such as tone of voice.

• 55 percent of communications—the most significant part—is a result of the person's physiology, including body language and facial expressions.[iii]

This highlights how building rapport through just words, manufactured common interests, and so on can be a loser's approach because it omits 93 percent of communications. To be skilled in building rapport with this other 93 percent, you need to have flexibility—meaning that you need to be attentive to the person you are communicating with in order to see how your message is being received, and then being adaptive enough to change your approach, if necessary. As discussed below, the key to building rapport involves you having enough variety, and range *in your own behavior* to match or pace with the other person. Some of the easiest and most effective ways to match and pace another individual are through:

- Physiology, or body language

- Speech patterns, including their rate of speech, tonality, volume, and select words

- Their lead representational system

The concept of pacing and matching was developed by the late clinical psychologist Milton Erickson. Essentially, the process involves mirroring the observable characteristics of the person you're meeting with. This phenomenon occurs naturally when people are in rapport. If, for example, you look around your favorite restaurant on a date night, you'll notice that a good number of couples will have a strikingly similar physical posture. By pacing and mirroring, you are *intentionally* creating rapport.[iv]

How to Mirror and Pace Physiology

In communications settings, an individual's physiology carries the greatest impact, a full 55 percent of the message. The physiological aspects of other people that you can mirror and pace include:

- Body posture, slumping over or sitting erect, standing up, crossing your legs, folding your arms or leaning forward, backward or to a particular direction.

- Body movements, including how you use of your hands, hand movements or gestures, or rocking in your seat.

- Facial expressions—such as smiles or a particular way of frowning.[v]

Related to pacing and matching physiology, there are similar ways to naturally take advantage of how a person uses their physical space. When you're sitting with people at home showing them a photo album or pictures on your iPhone, for example, you typically sit right next to them. This position naturally leads to a sharing of space, and better rapport. Likewise, in business meetings, those at a table will often sit directly opposite one another. A better rapport building spot would be to sit at the side of the table nearest to another person, so you aren't facing off.[vi]

A final note on pacing and mirroring physiology: in recent years, several books have been written about body language, attaching importance to various postures and gestures, such as crossed arms. In the approach for rapport discussed herein, it's not important to attribute any particular meaning to a person's posture, it's only important to be attentive to that individual's physiology, and then adjusting to it as appropriate.[vii]

How to Mirror or Pace Speech Patterns

As discussed above, 38 percent of communication is based on vocal expression, such as tone of voice. Among the items to consider matching and pacing are another individual's:

- Volume

- Tempo, or the pace and rhythm of the speech patterns

- Tone, or the pitch and frequency of the voice

- Timbre, or the individual characteristics and quality of the voice

- Word selection

- Voice inflection[viii]

Of course, certain aspects of one's voice should *not* be paced, particularly accents and stutters.

When you're on the phone with someone, vocal matching and pacing carries *far* more significance. Remember the statistics: 7 percent of communication is words, 38 percent voice. Consequently, the *way* the words are spoken ends up being five times more important than the words themselves. If we take these percentages and extrapolate them for phone use, that puts 82 percent of the onus on the voice and only 18 percent on the words. Folks might forget specific words in a telephone conversation, but they likely *won't* forget the feelings left behind through the way the words were communicated.

I've used vocal matching and pacing techniques often in building the nationwide practices I've been associated with. Frequently, my initial contact with another firm's exec occurs by telephone. My concentration on issues such as volume, vocal speed, and tone have led to a significant hit rate in establishing prospect meetings.

Many individuals find that rate of speech is the easiest thing to pace at first. For practice, it might make sense to start with a few people at work you know well. Listen to their speech rate and imitate it in your conversations with them. After a while, you'll find that you can do this without even thinking much about it.

Building Rapport with Elmer Milquetoast

A SALT-services professional I worked with named Greg

highlighted just how easy it is to learn and apply physiological and speech matching and pacing principles. A few days after studying such concepts, Greg and a teammate had a key meeting with an Ohio-based publicly-traded manufacturer that needed assistance on various sales-use examination issues and other services. The company's tax department contact was Elmer Milquetoast, a soft-spoken, mild guy, who soon sat hunched over with his hands folded at the conference room table. Thinking that unless they did something really fast, their meeting would be short and end unfruitfully, Greg remembered the matching and pacing approach he learned, and, before long, adopted Elmer's approximate posture and began to speak in a quiet voice. To their shock, within minutes Elmer warmed up to them, and the SALT teammates had an outstanding hour-long session in which they gained crucial insights. Two weeks after meeting Elmer, the SALT professionals were engaged on a six-figure-fee project, and believed their rapport techniques were an important aid in their success.

Will I Ever Get Caught and Upset Someone?

You might be thinking to yourself, "If I'm pacing and matching another person, won't they notice it?" Typically, most folks are so caught up in their own thoughts, or so self-consumed, it's very rare that they would notice your matching or pacing efforts, particularly in business settings. The key, of course, is to be gradual in your shifting of body posture, vocal characteristics, etc., versus robotically mimicking the other person.

Something Was Going On, But What?

A couple years back, one of my partners from Kentucky named Jose' was working on a project to create co-sourcing opportunities with smaller-public and large-private companies in Tennessee and Kentucky with Clive, a Cincinnati-based professional. Clive, was well-versed in unconscious rapport-building methods. A few months later, during a conference with Jose' and his managing partner Nell, Jose' was praising Clive's prospect-meeting skills, how he could dress-it-down when visiting with less sophisticated and good-ole-boy prospects, then dress-it-up in subsequent meetings during the day. He went on to say, "Clive's like a chameleon." What Jose' witnessed was Clive's flexibility to adjust his style and speak-the-prospect's language physiologically and verbally, and building compelling rapport.

Matching and Pacing a Lead Representation System

In addition to pacing or matching physiology and voice qualities, many professionals find that their level of rapport and persuasion can be expanded by pacing or matching a prospect or client's lead representation system. What's that? In western cultures, many people perceive the world and process information in one of three sensory systems: the visual, auditor, or kinesthetic sensory systems.[ix]

Individuals regularly use all three systems, but they normally have a preferred or lead representational system that they lean on most often. So, just as left-handed people are capable of, and do use, both hands, they are more dominant using one over the other. Clues exist to help you figure out another person's lead representation system. We'll focus on the most common and easiest to grasp: their verbal cues or predicates.

To pace or match a person's verbal cues or predicates, you need to be attentive to what to listen for, specifically, is the other person mainly using visual, auditory, or kinesthetic words or phrases? Once you've gleaned their more dominate or preferred representation system from their verbal cues or predicates, you'll want to speak the other person's language by talking to them in visual, auditory, or kinesthetic words. By adjusting your words to match the preference of your listener, you'll enhance rapport unconsciously.[x]

The key to pacing and matching verbal or auditory predicates, is to pay attention to a person's language cues, and adapt your style to that person's preferred language. Here are a handful of words and phrases that illustrate visual, auditory, and kinesthetic cues or predicates:

Visual Words and Phrases

Appear	Bright	Envision
Foggy	Glance	Hazy
Illuminate	Notice	Picture
See	Viewpoint	Watch
Look at this	Show me	Dark side

Auditory Words and Phrases

Articulate	Call	Chat
Describe	Discuss	Mention
Remark	Ring	Shout
Sounds like	Tell	Verbalize
Sounds good	Loud and Clear	Sing their praises

Kinesthetic Phrases

Absorb	Balance	Feel
Firm	Grasp	Rugged
Sense	Support	Tackle
Get a feel for	Go for it	I'm not comfortable

People who prefer visual language will use cues and predicates such as see, look, or picture, along with phrases such as illustrate a point, or do you see what I'm saying. To pace an individual's visual cues and predicates, simply respond using the identical language type. For example, if someone says, "Let's take a closer look at that issue," you'll want to respond with a phrase, such as, "Yes, let's see what's going on." For those with a visual lead representation system, graphs, pictures, or a PowerPoint presentation may enhance your meetings.

Individuals with a lead or dominant auditory representational system use cues such as hear or sounds like, and phrases such as sounds good to me or that rings true. Finally, those with a lead kinesthetic rep system use words such as feel and grasp, and phrases such as touch base or let's get our arms around this. Again, the mission for you is to match or pace their lead or preferred rep system.

There are many other methods to detect someone's dominate rep systems, with the foregoing verbal cues and predicates being the most user-friendly means.

You might be thinking to yourself, "How is this rapport stuff any more authentic then pretending I like antique farm equipment?" Well, in my view, it's *far* more genuine. Imagine for a moment that instead of being a CPA, you had a job at the International Terminal at O'Hare Airport in Chicago, and when a plane landed from Japan, you could speak Japanese to them, then when one arrived from Brazil, you could greet arriving passengers in Portuguese. By mastering these rapport skills, that's what you're developing—a communication tool providing you with the flexibility to speak to anyone.

Finally, some of you may think this process is too simplistic. If you're in that camp, I'd invite you to consider re-reading the section of Chapter 1 dealing with limiting beliefs.

As you'll see in future chapters, creating rapport is one of the key skills needed to succeed in developing your firm's business. Fortunately, this is an area you can get great at quickly with a little practice.

Listening to Win

Practically everyone has heard the expression, "God gave you two ears and one mouth, and that's a reflection of how much time you should listen versus talk." Perhaps that's a start. In many first meetings with prospects, you probably should be aiming for 75 to 80 percent listening. Unfortunately, many CPAs are so wanting to impress prospects with their intellect and knowledge, they'll do just the opposite, depriving themselves of a great opportunity to learn, and then persuade.

Fred Blows a Seven-figure Opportunity

The kids I grew up with on my block in downtown Gary, Indiana, ended up in a wide range of vocations, a couple of Catholic priests, two doctors, a Hollywood actor, a lawyer, many steelworkers and four CPAs, three of us becoming accounting firm partners. One of them named Ned ended up at a prominent super-regional firm on the west coast, and recently shared with me a classic story about listening.

Ned and one of his partners, Paula, generated a dream proposal opportunity with a high-profile Los Angeles-based investor in private companies that had grown tired of the handful of Big Four and national accounting firms that were auditing and providing tax services to their portfolio of businesses. They were perceived as being expensive and not particularly responsive. John, the executive sponsor at the L.A. prospect, had shared with Ned and Paula that he was comfortable with their firm as a sole-source provider to his portfolio of eleven entities, but that he wanted to work with a young, hungry partner or a senior manager, where the relationship would be a stepping-stone to partnership. John felt such a young, driven partner would give him and his portfolio of companies, undivided attention and outstanding service. Most of the portfolio was in the Pacific Northwest, with a couple firms in California.

Because their CPA firm was multi-office, with a strong presence in Washington, Idaho and Oregon, Ned and Paula involved Fred, a senior partner and national industry leader in commercial and industrial businesses who was in his late 50s, to help assess the situation. Fred had been well-schooled beforehand about John's strong preferences in terms of partner characteristics. He likewise was perceived by Ned and Paula to have connections and vision enough to identify the best potential client service partner in the organization to serve John and his team.

As the meeting started in Los Angeles with John, Ned, Paula, and Fred, Ned began by recapping prior meetings with John, and asked him if he could articulate for Fred's benefit their present CPA service situation, as well as what he was seeking for the future.

John got a few minutes into his overview, then Fred eagerly cut him off, hastily shouting, "I'll be your audit partner! I'll be your client services partner! I'll give you the very best service! You'll be our very best client! I'll shine your shoes after the meeting! I'll ...!" You get the picture.

Ned and Paula watched in horror as their firm's $1 million-plus potential fee opportunity slowly started swirling, then slide down the toilet bowl. Ned told me he thought he was going to have to peal Fred off John's leg if the meeting lasted much longer. Needless to say, Ned and Paula's hard work was all for naught.

Listening, Observing and Note-taking

Although Ned's story may seem a little extreme, I've personally witnessed and heard tales just like it, and perhaps you have, too. Paying complete attention to what your prospect is saying, and giving them a chance to fully convey their data, thoughts and opinions—without interruption—is not only critical to understanding your opportunity, but also a key way to improve rapport. Too often in these meetings, the CPA or advisor, like Fred, is busy thinking about what to say in response to the potential client, instead of relaxing and listening to what the prospect is noting.

In my experience, the most favorite person people like to talk about is themselves. So, once you've started your session with a great question to the prospect about their company and himself/herself, shut the pie hole, sit back, listen intently, take notes, and consider what the other person has to say. This approach likewise gives you a great chance to watch their physiology, and to adjust yours accordingly, building rapport. If you feel compelled to speak, say something such as, "How interesting." To the extent you interrupt the prospect's discussion with how you've solved, or seen such a problem before, or spend an inordinate amount of time talking about how great your firm (or you) are, the client will only hear, "Blah, blah, blah, blah, blah."

The Power of Quality Questions

I first was exposed to just how effective quality questions can be in social settings and in business meetings more than twenty years ago while reading Anthony Robbins' bestseller *Awaken the Giant Within*, and in his later *PowerTalk!* audio program series, *The Power of Questions*.[xi] In the intervening years, I've used, and watched my teammates avail well-crafted questions to discover game-changing thoughts and opinions prospects have held. Such incisive inquiries helped prospects clearly say what their real issues and challenges were. Consequently, that enabled us to bring ideas and solutions that were mutually beneficial.

Robbins asserts that the overall "process-of-thinking" most people undergo daily is nothing more than a progression of questions they ask themselves constantly. Such questions could be:

- What's going on right now?

- What does this mean to me? Is it good or bad? Will it cause me pain or pleasure?

- How should I act or respond?

He further stresses this is largely a habitual, unconscious process, and that these questions can direct us in a constructive way, or, drive our thinking into a ditch. Likewise, in business, he notes executives that regularly ask thoughtful, incisive questions about their markets, strategies, opportunities, or product and service lines are most apt to control their destiny.[xii]

Questions work personally, or in social and business settings three ways:

1. **Questions change what someone (or you) focuses on, and consequently their (or your) feelings.** For example, if someone is in a bad mood, simply asking, "What is exciting or great in your life now," where you ask the question congruently, or in a manner to get that person to seriously consider the question, often helps that person to think of experiences that might make them feel that way, or at a minimum, can help them break out of their crummy mood. You're not just psyching the person up, you're giving that person an opportunity to consider something empowering, along with helping him access some of the real reasons to feel those good feelings.[xiii]

2. **Questions change what someone (or you) are deleting.** As the above example illustrates, until someone asks what's exciting or great, all the exciting and great things in that person's life were being deleted. As highlighted above, your habitual questions, to yourself and others, serve as a laser beam of focus.

   One specific type of question that leads frequently to deletion is referred to as a presupposition question. Questions such as, "Why do I always screw up in prospect meetings?" or "Why can't I ever have the courage to make a cold call?" are perfect examples of negative and disempowering presupposition questions. In all likelihood, you don't *always*, probably not even frequently, screw up. The question's very nature results in you ignoring all the instances you did things well, or had the courage to make calls.[xiv]

3. **Questions have the potential to enhance and increase someone's (or your) available resources.** Structuring questions in a solutions-oriented way can lead others (and you) to

possibilities and answers, versus staying stuck. For example asking what your team can do today to identify those clients that aren't yet benefiting from your industry team's niche services, will likely begin to lead your group to the process of generating additional opportunities to stoke growth. You'll energize your team to find means to grow, versus just sitting-around.[xv]

Bringing this discussion full circle to Chapter 1's dialog on mindset, a crucial point is that *our beliefs affect the questions we'll even consider asking.* Some CPAs won't even contemplate how to master these influence, persuasion, and sales skills because bosses, co-workers, friends, or, maybe even a spouse, have told them it's impossible. They feel it's a waste of time and energy. Be careful to determine if you are the one creating limiting beliefs for others or asking limiting questions, or if your self-talk is full of limited questions. Remember, whether you believe you can or can't—you're right.[xvi]

Later, we'll explore specific types of questions that can help clarify ambiguous language and other high-impact questions you can use in prospect or proposal sessions to help identify what motivates a prospect. Now, we'll explore seven important words to regularly use in client and prospect sessions.

Magic Words

Kevin Hogan PhD a psychologist, is a thought-leader in the area of persuasion and influence having written 22 books on the subject. One of his YouTube videos highlights seven words of influence that may be useful to incorporate in your repertoire of language. These words are:

- **A person's first name.** When people hear their first name, it's normally music-to-their-ears. Consequently, it's important to get it right—calling someone by the wrong name can be a *real* rapport breaker. Further, being cognizant of whether the person prefers to be called by their given name or a nickname, is critical. According to Hogan, at a point, there is an inverse relationship between using a person's name and maintaining rapport. Using a person's name once or twice during a meeting is perfect, while repeated use of the person's name throughout a meeting can come across as annoying and be perceived as manipulative by the listener.[xvii]

- **Because.** Because can be a persuasive word in that it creates a "cause-and-effect linkage" to the listener. Linguistically, a listener in our culture is often influenced to follow a request that precedes the word because.[xviii] Harvard professor, psychologist and behavioral scientist Ellen Langer, PhD, and her colleagues, decided to put the persuasive power of this word to the test. In one study, Langer arranged for a stranger to approach someone waiting in line to use a photocopier and ask, "Excuse me, I have five pages, may I use the copy machine?" Faced with the direct request to cut ahead in this line, 60 percent of the people were willing to agree to allow the stranger to go ahead of them. However, when the stranger made the request with a *reason* 94 percent complied. When the stranger used the word because followed by completely meaningless reason, the rate of compliance was still 93 percent.[xix]

  In 1986, while Hogan was involved with the National Kidney Foundation, he tweaked telemarketer solicitation requests for fundraisers, adding the phrase, "**Because** it's really important," and found it increased contributions by nearly 30 percent.[xx]

- **Now**. According to Hogan, the word *now* has similar impact as the word because, although it features a command and requests action.[xxi] An example is, "Can we take a few moments and schedule our next appointment to gather data for our proposal now?"

- **Please and thank you.** Both mom and your grade school teachers were giving you great advice when they emphasized the need to say *please* and *thank you*.[xxii] It isn't surprising, though, that in today's quick response world, these words often aren't conveyed. According to Hogan's research, these expressions are enormously powerful, even though the listener knows the words are being used as an influencer by the speaker or writer to get a positive response. Using the word please to request a meeting seems like a pretty obvious courtesy, but thanking the person in advance can be a more elegant request.

  Note, *anytime* a prospect or referral source is gracious enough to meet with you, you should *always* follow up with a handwritten thank you note. You can do an e-mail to provide a quick thanks—but you still need to send the personal note of gratitude for the "gift of their time." This will *really* set you apart—for the better. In the last few years I've received several "thank-you-note e-mails" from recipients of my hand written thank you cards, noting how they were viewed as heartfelt and thoughtful . . . talk about cutting through today's clutter of communications.

- **Imagine.** The word *imagine* has a powerful impact because you're not telling someone what they need to do or should do, so the listener often gives little pushback. Hogan mentions that one of the Mercury Sable's most effective commercial lines in the 1990s was, "Imagine yourself driving a Mercury now!" which incorporated both imagine and now into the same ad.[xxiii] Your uses of the word imagine are limitless, and can include such statements as, "Imagine it's six months from now and you've cut your tax burden by $x,xxx,xxx because of the ideas we've helped you implement," or, "Imagine what it will be like next February when you're not working crazy hours because your CPA firm was unprepared. Won't that be a real positive change for you?"

- **Words or phrases signifying a listener's situational control.** Dr. Hogan believes that most people, especially business professionals, have a compelling need to feel they are in control of whatever it is going on around them, and, that absent that feeling, they sense risk or discomfort. Consequently, communications affirming the listener is in total control of a situation is persuasive to them. Conveying messages such as, *"You're the boss,"* or *"You're in charge,"* or *"You are in complete control of this,"* leads to favorable and empowering opinions for a listener.[xxiv]

Now, let's focus on the sloppy messages we encounter in our daily lives, and how to sharpen our understanding of what others are really trying to say to us.

Basic Language Patterns

Often during prospect or proposal-related meetings, or other times where you are needing to be influential, you invest considerable time gathering information from others. Even though you have mastered rapport skills, these meetings may not be completely tension free and the people you're with may use vague or general language. To be effective, you need to understand precisely what someone is saying to you, by boiling down the junky language that others use day-in, day-out. This language clarification process is based on a set of NLP tools developed in the mid-1970s called the Meta Model. The process first requires you to be listening for vague or non-specific words. Then, depending on the context and relative importance of that information, asking specific clarifying questions. Through your listening and inquiries, you'll be able to generate a crystal-clear understanding of the prospect's issues and circumstances, which then allows you to solve problems and increase your influence.

Junky or vague language often takes one of three forms:

- Only some information is conveyed and a great deal is left out or deleted.

- An overly simplified account or explanation is provided, which can potentially distort the message.

- Generalized information is provided, because expressing every condition would make the conversation lengthy and tedious.[xxv]

The Meta Model questioning process seeks to reverse and unravel the deletions, distortions, and generalizations of a communicator's language. Five categories of such language patterns are common in the CPA world.

Unspecified Nouns

How often have you heard someone say:

- "**They** don't understand me?"

- "**They** are not doing their job."

Well, just who are "they?" If it's a big organization, there is likely one, specific person who is being referred to. So instead of getting stuck in vagueness, find a way to deal with the real-world person. In this context, the word "they" is referred to as an unspecified noun. If you are speaking with someone and don't know who "they" are, you are likely unable to be helpful or influential.[xxvi]

Junky language involving unspecified nouns can be cleaned up by simply asking who or which.[xxvii] Let's look at a few examples:

Unspecified People, Places, and Things	Meta Model Inquiry
"Those advisors are really inconsiderate."	"Which advisors, specifically?"
"All those year-end things are *really* getting me down."	"Which things, specifically?"
"The powers that be want us to make an auditor change."	"Who are they?"
"They rejected the planning idea you recommended."	"Who specifically?"

Oh, Yes. The Importance of Softeners

The above Meta Model questions can easily become annoying, particularly where someone uses a quick, harsh or angry tone, or if they've asked the questions in a rapid-fire succession. Unfortunately, many use these types of questions *precisely when they are* in a poor frame of mind. One way to temper your use of Meta Model questions, is to precede the question with a softening phrase such as:

- "Can you tell me which person specifically?"

- "I'd truly love to know . . . "

- "Can you give me an example of how . . .?"

- "I am curious . . . "

- "I'm wondering . . . "

• "Perhaps you may know . . . "

Using these softener phrases will make your clarifying questions come across *much* more elegantly.

Nominalizations

What do words like independence, responsiveness and attention have in common? They are all nouns, yes, but can you find them in the real world? Have you ever seen "a responsiveness?" It's not a person, place, or thing. Nominalizations involve verbs, or action words that have been transformed into nouns— in the case the verb "respond" (describing the process of responding), was converted into the noun "responsiveness."

When you hear a nominalization, a great way to get clarification of what a person is actually saying, is to turn the word back into a process. If a prospect said that having a *relationship* is a key factor in selecting a CPA firm, you might ask how he or she want to relate to the firm. Other examples include:

Nominalization Statement	How You Turn the Nominalization into a Process
"Our **experience** with tax advisors has been poor."	"What do you want to experience?"
"I'm expecting regular **attention** from our CPA firm."	"Could you clarify how to best attend to . . . ?"
"We are looking for **creativity** with our partner."	"What do you want to create?"

Nominalizations can be pretty slimy. In fact, vocations where you can hear them used daily involve the government and politicians—

think of words like equality, freedom, safety, and prosperity. In CPA proposal settings, an accountant/listener can erroneously attach a variety of meanings to a nominalization, because their definitions of characteristics like experience, attention, and relationship are potentially *very* different from a client's or prospect's meaning. Consequently, it's worth the effort to identify that gist in persuasion-related settings, because if you don't know what someone really wants, you'll not be able to deliver.

Universal Quantifiers

Words such as all, none, every, always, and never are known as universal quantifiers.[xxviii] Universal quantifiers are fine when they are true. If you say that *every* person needs oxygen or *all* the accounting professors at Indiana University have graduated from college, you are merely conveying facts.[xxix] Most of the time, however, when someone is using a universal quantifier, they are over generalizing and not seeing exceptions. An example is *all* CPAs are geeks. When you hear a universal quantifier, you can challenge the generalization with questions, such as:

- "*All* CPAs?"

- "You're saying that every single CPA you've ever met in your entire life has been a total geek?"

- "Have you ever met a CPA who wasn't?"

Restrictive Words — Modal Operators of Necessity and Impossibility

Modal operators of necessity are words like should and should not, must and must not, ought and ought not, and required. Use of these words indicates that there is some rule of conduct the person is operating by, but the rule is not explicit. To help you in a persuasion setting, you'd like to understand what the consequences are (whether they're real or imagined), of breaking the rule. These can be clarified by asking *what* would happen if you did, or did not, do something."[xxx] Examples you might hear include:

- "We *shouldn't* meet with you because we already work with Bob Williams, CPA."

- "It's already September, we *ought not* go out for audit or tax proposals for this year end."

- "I know you've already provided us with compelling reasons to make a change to your firm, but *we're required* to get at least three proposals."

By asking the aforementioned question, the consequences and reasons are made explicit, and they can be thought over and critically evaluated, otherwise they just limit your party's choices and behavior.[xxxi]

Modal operators of impossibility have stronger implications because they involve words such as couldn't, cannot or can't, and impossible. These words often identify the limits set by a person's beliefs.[xxxii] Common statements might include:

- "We *can't* use a regional firm for our annual audits."

- "It's *not possible* for us to separate advisors for tax versus audit services."

- "We *couldn't possibly* change our tax accounting method for this year."

When you are gathering information or attempting to persuade someone voicing a modal operator of impossibility, great questions include:

- "What would happen if you did?"

- "What stops you?"

- "How do you stop yourself?"

- "What would it be like if you could?"

Typically, when you are speaking with those who say that they can't do something, they have set up an outcome and put it out of reach. Asking a question such as, "What stops you?" puts emphasis on the outcome again and starts a process to identify barriers, which is frequently the first step to getting past them.[xxxiii]

Clean Up Your Stinking But and Why

Our emphasis in this chapter has been on building rapport and clarifying communications with others to enable you to better influence and persuade. There is one additional fine point involving language for you to keep in mind.

Consider the connective words *but, and,* and *even though*. When you link ideas or experiences together, substituting each one of these three different words will lead your listener to focus attention on a distinct part of the message. If you tell someone, "You are doing a great job **but** you need to focus on _____," it will lead the listener to concentrate more on what he or she needs to focus on, and less on what they are doing well. If someone connects the same two thoughts with the word *and,* they are equally emphasized. If you use *even though* to connect two thoughts, the effect is to focus the listener's attention more on the first part of the statement.

Many people have a habitual pattern in which they dismiss either positive commentary or ideas with the word "but." If you want to be a rapport champion, *get the word but out of your vocabulary*.

Another word to delete from your vocabulary is *why*, particularly in influence or persuasion settings. Putting your inquiries in a *why format* can be construed as accusatory, potentially leading your audience to feel defensive. You can replace your whys with inquiries such as:

- "What was your motivation for . . .?"

- "How did you . . . ?"

- "What led you to . . .?"

Now that you know precisely how to figure out what prospects and others want, it makes sense for you to know what you want, too, by using the power of goal setting.

Goal Setting

Goal setting and getting are such incredibly important topics that dozens of terrific books and audio programs have been authored on the subject. Among my favorites are Napoleon Hill's 1937 classic *Think & Grow Rich*, in which Hill unveils the "science of personal achievement" through study of the early titans of American business; David J. Schwartz's *The Magic of Thinking Big*; and Anthony Robbins' *Personal Power II* program, a 30-day mental diet for realizing success in life. Each made major contributions to my overall accomplishments, thought processes, and business philosophy. With such powerful resources available for you, I'll limit discussion on goal setting to a handful of key points, and let you dig into these master works for more detail.

The goal setting method I've observed at many CPA firms is mostly a halfhearted process. Annual goals read more like production requirements set by professionals and their bosses for the next 12 months: "You will have X-number of chargeable hours, achieve realization of Y-%, join the such and such charitable board, and keep unbilled work-in-process under $-Z." With such impotent, inwardly-focused aspirations, it's no wonder there is limited innovation and mediocre growth in large part within the industry. Budgets and work-related expectations are a great thing— just don't confuse them with inspiring goals that will move the needle for most individuals or your firm.

How Goal Setting Works

Remember the last time you purchased a new car, and started driving it around town? All of the sudden, you started seeing all the smart people who had the same great taste in vehicles as you, cruising through town. Similarly, a pregnant woman will start noticing and observing other expecting women. Were the cars and pregnant women there before, or simply not things you paid attention to?

What is it that's provoking your awareness? At the base of the brain, the point that connects to the spinal cord, is a brain region known as the reticular activating system (RAS). It's sometimes referred to as the brain's brain. The RAS acts like a TV station's news editor, because editors make decisions on which stories get coverage and treated as breaking news, and which stories wind up being buried.

The RAS receives thousands of messages each second. Everything you see, hear, smell, feel, and touch is a message that enters your brain. The RAS filters through all these messages and decides which ones will get TV airplay—that is, arouse the brain.

The RAS can be intentionally stimulated during the goal-setting process. Specifically, by keeping your desired goal consciously in the forefront of your mind, you'll fuel your RAS to notice means and methods for attaining the outcome. So, once you've decided a goal's realization is a priority, give it emotional intensity, and continually focus on it becoming real, resources that support its manifestation will start to become clear, often seemingly from nowhere!

Points on Goal Setting and Getting

Here are a few points to consider when setting achievable goals:

- Your goals *absolutely* need to be in writing, otherwise they are simply a hope or dream.

- In structuring goals, they need to have process-related elements to them. A goal to create $250,000 in net new revenue for the next 12 months would contain processes that could be accomplished and measured regularly. So, in achieving this $250K growth outcome, you'd want to establish sub-goals for weekly prospect calls or visits, and for projects to be identified from mining opportunities with existing clients and so on.

- Goals need to have a completion date or deadline, otherwise procrastination can kick in.

- Once you've set a goal, identify at least one action step that you can do within the first 24-hours to get some momentum, even if it's something simple like ordering a topical book online.

- You should read aloud your most important goals, or find a way to otherwise stimulate your RAS daily. A methodology I've used for the past 15-years or so involves creating a goal map of my most important outcomes—and hanging the goal map in my office at work and exercise room at home. An example goal map follows on the next page. Some of you might view this approach as over-the-top, or even be concerned what co-workers might think of you, but many high-achievers have used this process with amazing results. You simply can't be worried about what others think about your desire to succeed.

An example goal map

- To the extent your desired goal is complex, such as starting a new business unit within your shop, the goal will likely require the creation of a more detailed plan with process-related action steps and timelines. There are many exceptional books and study-at-home programs to provide you with the ABCs of strategy to accomplish this.

- Stay true to your goal, even though you may need or want to change your roadmap to achieve it. Once you roll up your sleeves and get into the thick of perusing your goal, certain tactics and strategies may not work, so be flexible in your approach. Don't abandon the overall goal, though.

• Learn from others, and potentially model them. On several occasions when I've commenced new business units, I'd find someone in a completely different part of the U.S. that had a similar, but non-competing business and talk to them, or visit them personally to learn more about their practice. Frequently, they were quite generous with their time. In some cases, I'd pay them for their education, or trade something of value expertise-wise as compensation. Bottom-line, it can save you months or even years of time, help your firm and you avoid costly mistakes, and potentially create a relationship to lean on in the future.

• Irrespective of your goal's overall success, what many people find is just the process of setting and pursuing a worthy goal generates *tremendous* personal growth and learning. You will likely have much more value as a person and professional by your having engaged in this process.

For some, many of the personal skills we've discussed in Chapter 2 may be brand new to you, and consequently awkward as you first try them out. Mindful that many folks simply give up when something isn't comfortable, let's highlight one of the most critical personal characteristics in overall achievement—and in influence, persuasion and sales.

The Power of Grit

Grit. It's truly one of those characteristics for you to nurture in order to attain the success you deserve in life. Just so we're on the same page, let's define grit, and what many thought leaders in the area of human achievement have observed about its role versus other traits, such as intelligence.

Grit is described as having a tenacious, passionate, and enduring pursuit towards a long-term goal. It's sticking with a future objective in order to make it happen. It involves living your life, and pursuing a dream as if it is a marathon, versus a sprint. Many view it as the elixir for achievement and success when a person otherwise lacks talent or other resources.[xxxiv]

Over the past 10 years or so, multiple books have been penned comparing the relative value of grit versus I.Q., and research strongly suggests that the link between smarts and achievement isn't nearly as related as once thought.[xxxv] In a recent interview of leading University of Pennsylvania behavioral psychologist Angela Lee Duckworth, PhD, Duckworth noted that, "On average, grittier people turn out to be more successful than others, particularly in very challenging situations . . . We have a solid base of research on the importance of grit, and are now transitioning into research on how to build grit."[xxxvi]

In her book, *Mindsets—How We Can Learn to Fulfill Our Potential*, Stanford University psychologist Carol Dweck, PhD describes characteristics of individuals possessing a "growth mindset," a view that a person's ability is changeable through learning (a key ingredient in grittier people), as opposed to those having a "fixed mindset," defined as an outlook where aptitude is static, and success is about proving yourself by showing how smart or talented you are to validate yourself. Where the person with grit and a growth mindset will view a setback such as losing-out on a key audit or tax proposal as an indication that they need to improve their influence, persuasion and sales-related skills; fixed-mindset individuals will likely view themselves as basically being "awful-at-sales." Dweck points out that growth and fixed mindsets are just beliefs, which can be changed.[xxxvii]

This notion of how one's ability and talent can be positively transformed through a deliberate learning process, has been documented physiologically via the study of brain neuroplasticity. Specifically, in *The Mind and The Brain—Neuroplasticity and the Power of Mental Force*, Dr. Jeffrey Schwartz and Sharon Begley state that, "Conscious thoughts and volitions can, and do, play a powerful causal role in the world, including influencing the activity on the brain . . . Sensory stimulation reaching the brain can result not only in one region of the brain colonizing another with remarkable effects on mental and physical function but in the wholesale remodeling of neural networks."[xxxviii] In other words, focused learning, desire and will, the grit you cultivate, actually changes your brain's connections and makes you more resourceful!

Ways to Develop Grit

Although, as Dr. Duckworth noted, the research is still evolving, select psychologists currently view the following as techniques to help develop the trait of grit.

- **Goal setting:** Identify goals that are most critical to you, and then, get at them.

- **Practice regularly:** What you need to rehearse and practice are activities designed to improve definite phases of your performance. Specifically, concentrate on those weaknesses that are critical to an aspect of success.[xxxix] If building vocal rapport skills are a goal for you for example, practice your matching and pacing skills on *all* calls, not just on cold calls to set appointments.

- **Learn how to be optimistic:** In Martin Seligman's 1990 bestseller *Learned Optimism*, Seligman observed that sales professionals with an optimistic, explanatory style outsold pessimists by more than 30 percent after the first training year. Per Seligman, an optimist has features similar to the growth mindset persona, and pessimists possess the characteristics of the fixed mindset individual. Further, optimists view setbacks as temporary, whereas pessimists believe they are pervasive.[xl]

• **Expect challenges**[xli]: Being able to maintain grit in the face of inevitable problems requires a person to anticipate difficulties arising, choosing alternative responses for them, and, where possible, practicing methods to handle them.[xlii]

• **Avoid distractions and stay focused:** It goes without saying that we're in a world of devices and information overload, so keeping on task is part of the heart of building grit.

Rob Wagner—the Story of One Gritty CPA

Everyone, at some point of time in their career, works with a co-worker that is SO GOOD they make you look far more talented than you really are. For me, that guy is Rob Wagner, an international tax partner at BKD, LLP, and a truly gritty CPA.

I had been working to recruit a new tax partner for Olive's Ft. Wayne practice in the spring of 1996, and was networking with Indianapolis-based professionals to see who we could possibly convince to come to northeast Indiana. We likewise were searching for an international tax leader to incubate a practice, mainly with out-of-market folks, since there were no real international candidates in the Indianapolis metro area at the time. I spoke with Rob, who was on the partner candidate list at Price Waterhouse & Co. with the Ft. Wayne opportunity in mind, but he, along with support from his wife Christie, said he'd be interested in retooling to become an international tax specialist at Olive, in Indianapolis if that were a possibility.

His progression to international tax excellence was one of those grinding processes that included:

• Being individually tutored by a prominent international tax law school professor for 2-years.

- Gathering up and centralizing all international tax services work for the firm under him.

- Creating a network with skilled U.S. international tax attorneys to discuss practical issues that arose.

- Crafting a system of foreign tax advisors throughout the world to provide in-country tax advisory.

- Participating in multiple high-level CPE courses in the international services arena.

- Countless hours of self-study and international travel to strengthen technical skills and relationships.

Rob took a huge leap-of-faith with Olive in 1996, jumping-in with both feet to master the subject matter, and over time building what is now BKD's impressive ITS practice, a practice that now has three partners and a managing director, and is a real middle-market differentiator for the firm. All made possible with Rob Wagner's talent—and grit.

My High School Reunion—and Your Pathway Forward

I recently attended my 40th high school reunion in lovely Gary, IN, along with my wife and former classmate, Ellen. For reunions it was fairly well attended, with roughly 90 folks from our 270-member graduating class journeying back to the Steel City. At first, I wondered who invited all these old-looking folks to our celebration, but soon realized they were my contemporaries from 1974.

Through the night's merriment, Ellen and I observed compelling differences in our fellow student's lives. Some appeared to be in sub-par health, looking like they packed on 100 pounds or so, whereas others remained fit. A handful noted that they had just retired, feeling comfortable with their accumulated lifetime wealth, while some openly said they didn't know how they'd ever afford retirement. Many seemed happy in their lives and relationships, but a few expressed bitterness. Most seemed to live fairly sober lives, although one bragged he smoked pot every day for the last 40-years, as if he had achieved some notable milestone like Joe DiMaggio's 56-game hitting streak.

What my high school reunion truly exemplified is how the choices we make, and actions taken through time, have a *profound* impact on where we ultimately end up. As the late entrepreneur, author, and motivational speaker, Jim Rohn, would say, "Success is nothing more than a few simple disciplines, practiced every day. And, failure is not a single, cataclysmic event, just a few errors in judgment, repeated every day."[xliii]

I love the CPA industry's professionals, and am passionate about seeing you and your firm enjoying even more success now. Further, I strongly believe accounting firms and the professionals at such firms can *dramatically* change the trajectory of their results, for the good, with effective education, strategy, execution, and perseverance. It doesn't matter now if you have five, 10, 20, or 30 years left in your CPA career, your dedication to mastering the principles from this chapter will *make an incredible difference* in the years to come!

Chapter 2 References

[i]Hess, Alexander E.M.; Calio, Vince; Frohlich, Thomas C. *Nine Countries That Hate America Most.* 24/7wallst.com. April 10, 2014

[ii]The NLP Comprehensive Training Team—edited by Andreas, Steve and Faulkner, Charles. *NLP—The New Technology of Achievement.* Quill, William Morrow. New York, NY, 1994. Pages 83-84

[iii]O'Conner, Joseph; Seymour, John. *Introducing NLP Neuro-Linguistic Programming*. Thorsons Publishing. Hammersmith London, England, 1995. Pages 17-18

[iv]The NLP Comprehensive Training Team, op. cit., Pages 149-150

[v]Ibid. Pages 149-150

[vi]Ibid. Page 153

[vii]Brooks, Michael. *Instant Rapport*. Warner Books, Inc. New York, NY, 1989. Page 140

[viii]The NLP Comprehensive Training Team, op. cit., Pages 150-153

[ix]O'Conner, op. cit., Pages 25-39

[x]Ibid. Pages 25-39

[xi]Robbins, Anthony. *Awaken the Giant Within*. Summit Books, New York, NY 1991. Robbins, Anthony. *PowerTalk! The Power of Questions*. Robbins Research International, Inc. San Diego, CA, 1993.

[xii]Ibid. Pages 187-188

[xiii]Ibid. Pages 194-197

[xiv]Ibid. Pages 197-199

[xv]Ibid. Pages 199-201

[xvi]Ibid. Pages 200-201

[xvii]Hogan, Kevin. *Magic Words of Persuasion with Kevin Hogan*. YouTube Kevin Hogan Channel. April 3, 2009 (10:52).

[xviii]Ibid.

[xix]Cowen, Tyler. *The Power of Because*. MarginalRevelotion.com. June 25, 2008.

[xx]Hogan, op. cit.

[xxi]Ibid.

[xxii]Ibid.

[xxiii]Ibid.

[xxiv]Ibid.

[xxv]NLP Comprehensive. *NLP Comprehensive Practitioner Certification Training Course Materials*. NLP Comprehensive, Boulder, CO, 1999. Page 3-1

[xxvi]Robbins, Anthony. *Unlimited Power*. Ballantine Books, New York, NY, 1986. Page 225

xxviiNLP Comprehensive, op. cit. Page 3-2

xxviiiIbid. Page 3-5

xxixRobbins, op. cit. Page 223

xxxO'Conner, op. cit. Pages 98-99

xxxiIbid. Page 98

xxxiiIbid. Pages 96-97

xxxiiiIbid. Page 97

xxxivDuckworth Ph.D., Angela Lee. *The Key to Success? Grit.* YouTube—Filmed at TED Talks Education. April, 2013 (6:12).

xxxvColvin, Geoff. *Talent is Overrated—What Really Separates World-Class Performers from Everyone Else.* Penguin Group, New York, NY, 2013. Page 45

xxxviStains, Laurence Roy. "Got Grit?" *Men's Health Magazine*, October, 2014. Page 154

xxxviiDweck Ph.D., Carol S. *Mindset—How We Can Learn to Fulfill Our Potential.* Ballantine Books, New York, NY, 2006. Pages 15-16

xxxviiiSchwartz, M.D., Jeffrey M.; and Begley, Sharon. *The Mind and the Brain—Neuroplasticity and the Power of Mental Force.* HarperCollins Publishers, Inc., New York, NY, 2002. Pages 16-17

xxxixStains, op. cit. Page 154

xlSeligman, Ph.D., Martin E.P. *Learned Optimism—How to Change Your Life and Mind.* Pocket Books, New York, NY, 1990. Pages 101, 104 and 255

xliStains, op. cit. Page 155

xliiDuhigg, Charles. *The Power of Habit—Why We Do What We Do in Life and Business.* Random House Publishing Group, New York, NY, 2012. Pages 145-147

xliiiRohn, Jim. *The Art of Exceptional Living.* Simon & Schuster Audio—a Nightingale-Conant Production, 1994.

CHAPTER 3

A LITTLE SOCIAL PSYCHOLOGY
YOU SHOULD UNDERSTAND

Just as many animals have instinctual behaviors when they encounter a trigger event in their habitats, human beings likewise are prone to act in certain ways when specific social stimuli or conditions are present. One of the all-time great books on these social psychology principles, and how they are activated in everyday life, is Robert B. Cialdini's bestseller *Influence—The Psychology of Persuasion*, a paperback you should *definitely* have in your library.

In the animal kingdom, polecats, a weasel-like species, are considered to be predatory to turkeys, and a maternal turkey will tear into shreds a toy stuffed polecat that is placed in her territory. On the other hand, to the extent the stuffed polecat toy is equipped with a sound device that makes the chirping sounds of a baby turkey, the polecat model will be nurtured and mothered by the maternal bird, with the physical traits of the presumed killer being completely ignored by the turkey.[i]

Similarly, humans are strongly impacted by select social influencers. In the preceding chapter we highlighted Dr. Ellen Langer's experiments showing how the word *because* swayed subjects to comply with a rather ridiculous request. Cialdini's studies involve how social phenomenon, like the rule of reciprocity,

59

consistency and commitment, social proof, liking, authority, and scarcity have a strong impact on an individual's compliance with the wishes of others. These social persuaders, notwithstanding their power, frequently do not garner much advanced attention by those they impact, and thus, the six are often called non-conscious influencers. As a result, these principles have been smuggled by some, and used unethically. We'll of course, discuss means to employ these doctrines honorably.

The Rule of Reciprocity

"Essentially the rule of reciprocity stands for the notion that we as individuals should attempt to repay in kind whatever someone provides to us—obligating us to repay a multitude of gestures, gifts, invitations, and niceties."[ii] This principle arises cross-culturally, and there are genuine stigmas and harsh labels for those that have received some benefit under the rule, but fail to give back. Folks fitting that description are called unflattering names such as ingrates, takers and freeloaders. Consequently, the rule of reciprocity carries considerable pull, and the perceived obligation one feels under this tenet oftentimes causes a person to do things they otherwise wouldn't have done.[iii]

Cialdini notes that one of the social purposes of the rule, "Was to promote the development of reciprocal relationships between individuals so that one person could initiate acts, without having a fear of loss," meaning, the uninvited favor must be able to create an obligation.[iv] As noted above, the obligation to repay is the essence of the rule, however, the foregoing implicit *duty to receive favors or gifts* provides an opening to exploiters. Such a manipulative example cited by Cialdini involves the Krishna's of the late 1970s and early 1980s, a ploy I was personally sucked into with my wife on our honeymoon in Hawaii.

In the 1970s, the Hare Krishna Society, a religious organization, performed fundraising in places like airports, such as Chicago's O'Hare. In their approach, the Krishna provided a book or flower to unsuspecting individuals, telling them it was a gift from the Krishna Society. Once accepted, the donor would not take the gift back under any condition, but, if the recipient would like to make a financial contribution to continue the good works of the Society, that would be much appreciated. This abuse of the reciprocation rule generated spectacular growth for the Society in terms of wealth, but eventually resulted in their fundraising being banned in various settings—with courts later upholding such prohibitions. The blowback from these shortsighted tactics, was a dramatic drop in U.S. fundraising, ultimately leading to the closure of a huge number of their religious centers. Nevertheless, the Krishna Society's approach illustrates how small gifts and favors can create uneven exchanges, as well as the shrewd power of this rule.

Cialdini likewise explores how "reciprocal concessions" constitute a form of this principle.[v] In other words, to the extent an individual makes a concession to us, we feel pressure to make a concession to them in tradeoff. In our CPA world, we see this in IRS examinations, particularly where the case moves on to the administrative or appeals level. Generally, appeals cases involve one or many high-dollar issues where the examining IRS agent and you initially agreed-to-disagree with the tax treatment of an item(s). The appeals agent, in many circumstances provides some compromise based on the government's alleged hazards of litigation. In many cases, the concession by the IRS, even where not optimal, is frequently reciprocated by your acceptance of the Service's proposal.

Cialdini's research shows how reciprocal concessions have been used effectively in sales circumstances, too. For example,

Brunswick Corporation's pool table division found that where its sales professionals showed customers higher-priced units first, followed by lower-priced tables, customers' overall purchases were for a higher dollar amount. In other words, they conceded by acquiring the next highest-priced pool table. Furthermore, other research showed that where customers refused to buy a product or service, they were often willing to refer potential clients to the sales professional, as part of a reciprocal concession.[vi]

Here is an example of how one of my former teams unwittingly brought the reciprocity principle into use favorably. Several years ago, I came across Gary Vaynerchuk's book *Crush It! Why NOW Is the Time to Cash In on Your Passion*, and was intrigued by Vaynerchuck's use of video for marketing purposes.[vii] Among other techniques, he used a video program he dubbed Wine Library TV to help grow a wine and spirits retailer his father owned, from roughly $2 million dollars in revenue to more than $50 million in receipts. I perceived this could be a novel way to help heighten brand recognition for the relatively young private equity firm-focused transaction services practice we had started in the midst of the financial crises. After much debate, BKD launched Private Equity TV, or PE TV, where we interviewed thought leaders from select private equity firms, and other professionals with neat ideas that could assist PE firms. We would typically dialogue with one of the firm's key partners about what made their firm special, and why they were a great partner to engage with in a transaction. The end-product film was electronically shipped out to 15,000 business owners, investment banks, PE firms, and others that were tangential to deals. Further, we allowed the interviewee's firm to use the videos for their marketing or other purposes.

Surprisingly, what we discovered is that many of the firms we featured on PE TV later hired us to perform financial diligence services on a deal. Although we'd like to believe our relentless marketing efforts, sales skills, and transactional expertise contributed to these successes—some of us clearly felt the reciprocity principle had a role in getting our team to the table to begin with, even though that was not the driving force for interviewing a specific PE group.

Cialdini believes that many business people fail to properly gather reciprocity-rule-chits to avail in the future. Many professionals, including CPAs, perform Herculean tasks on behalf of clients from time to time. Things like working multiple weekends or significant overtime to meet deadlines. Clients, recognizing the extraordinary effort that was put in, might heap-on praise or compliment you with an effusive *thank you* for the well-done task. What will the professional, or CPA say in response? Generally, they'll say something like, "Oh, it was no big deal," or, "Well, it's just all part of my job you know," bungling the reciprocity opportunity. Instead, he advises you to acknowledge the compliment, and couple it with a follow-on statement, such as, "Wow, thank you for recognizing our team's hard work. I'm *sure you'd do the same for us.*" Cialdini theorizes the italicized segment of such response can obligate the listener under the reciprocity rule (i.e., for future favors).[viii]

What are some other potential opportunities to avail reciprocity in a CPA firm environment? A few options might include:

- Hosting periodic roundtable events sponsored by your firm with key client or prospective-client executives within an industry, such as local energy industry executives or banking leaders, to discuss specific industry-related issues.

- Providing complimentary tax physicals for non-clients to identify savings opportunities.

- Offering to assist with certain high-value consulting-related services for a prospect, but low-dollar cost to your firm. Certain automatic accounting method changes could fall into this category.

Certainly, you and your team can brainstorm even more ways to ethically use this principle within your practice.

Consistency and Commitment

Behaving in a manner consistent with a commitment previously made is a powerful influencer. Further, most have an almost obsessive desire to be consistent with something they've already said or done. According to Cialdini's research, "Once we've made a choice or have taken a stand, we have personal and 'interpersonal pressure' to be consistent with that commitment (i.e., to justify our choice)."[ix]

In our culture, acting consistently is a highly valued personality trait. In contrast, we say nasty things about those who behave in an inconsistent fashion, calling them wishy-washy or, worse, liars. Media outlets likewise love to uncover the hypocrisy of politicians that commit this type of sin. Think back on how President George H. W. Bush was crucified politically when he backed-off his 1988 campaign pledge of, "Read my lips, no new taxes!" arguably costing him the 1992 election. Likewise President Obama's, "If you like your plan, you can keep your healthcare plan legislation promise," has landed him in deep trouble with many Americans. In short, where you can get someone to take a stand or go on the record with a view or commitment, there is an enormous amount of social pressure to act consistently with that position or promise.[x]

One of the more notorious uses of this commitment and consistency influencer occurred during the Korean War and the treatment of U.S. POWs in Chinese prison camps during the 1950s.

The so-called lenient policy employed by the Chinese treated POWs as victims of the U.S. ruling classes, and they were given sufficient food and proper medical treatment in captivity. They were neither robbed nor abused by the captors. Instead they were coaxed towards an understanding of the true nature of the war in the communist Chinese view, and of the ills of the U.S. After re-education, prisoners were either released at the war's front to rejoin and demoralize their old units, or used to gather intelligence from other prisoners at the camp, collaborating with the enemy.[xi]

For these POWs, the process normally began after a friendly gesture by a captor, maybe something as simple as being given a cigarette. The captor would then ask the POW a simple question, "Are there any things that are wrong with the U.S.?" The POW might mumble a few things, then a few minutes later, the Communist captor would ask the POW if he'd write down those problems with America on a piece of paper, and sign his name to it. The POW would often hesitate, yet any reluctance would be broken by the Chinese by reminding the POW, he did in fact, just say that these various things were wrong about America. Later in the day, the head of the camp would then get on a loudspeaker and read the written confession or note to all prisoners. Fellow prisoners would confront the apparent traitor, asking what was going on and why he would say such negative things about the U.S. Frequently, the collaborator's response, due to the social pressure of consistency and commitment would blurt out, "Because it's true!" This unassuming process caused troublesome conflict among the U.S. captives.

The research on consistency and commitment concludes that this influencer is most effective when the promise or pledge is active, public, effortful and internal (i.e., made without strong outside pressure or a significant reward).

Business-wise, there are several ways to *constructively elicit consistency and commitment* as a tool for influence, including:

- **Sales-related goal setting:** Having teammates individually write down their goals, then reading and discussing them as part of an office or industry team strategy meeting to bolster follow through on the goal.

- **Case studies:** Hopefully there are many instances each year where you have helped a client save money with a business or tax planning idea, identified means for them to streamline processes that save personnel time, or alternatively lessened their business risks with other thoughtful advice. Each and every time this occurs, capturing that win via a case study, which the client approves and signs-off on, is an exceptional way to memorialize the client's acknowledgement of your excellence. The case study obviously helps bind commitment to your firm and you. We'll also highlight the importance of having these case studies under the "Social Proof" section of this chapter below.

- **Reference calls:** During new engagement proposals, having your well-satisfied existing clients proactively make reference calls to the prospect prior to the prospect's request for references, distinguishes your firm to the prospective client, and likewise helps bind your existing client to your firm via this principle.

- **Client referrals:** Obtaining referral opportunities from existing clients is certainly efficient and effective for business development purposes, and can create a commitment affect similar to reference calls.

- **Starter projects:** Getting a starter project with a new prospect, and knocking it out of the park with your performance, is an excellent method to bridge into bigger and better engagements under the consistency and commitment norm.

Let's shift gears now to another social psychology influencer that we can readily access in the CPA world, the power of . . .

Social Proof

Social proof relates to an individual's tendency to follow the crowd. According to Cialdini, "One means used to determine what is 'correct' involves finding out what other people think is 'correct.' When individuals see a sufficient number of others engaged in a behavior, it's assumed as proper for the situation. Generally, folks believe they will make fewer mistakes—and more right choices by acting in accord with social evidence, than contrary to it."[xii] In short, many individuals feel that reliance on social proof expedites the process of decision making and leads to better overall decisions.

In the business world, consumer-related companies tout when their products or services are growing rapidly, because they don't have to necessarily convince you that their offering is the best— simply by showing you that everyone else thinks the product/ service is great (e.g., by its robust sales), typically is proof enough for you too.[xiii]

Social proof conditions are most ripe when people are unsure of themselves, or when there is a great degree of ambiguity and uncertainty. When people are in a heightened feeling or state of uncertainty about conditions, they are more apt to accept the behaviors of the others as correct.[xiv]

One of the more tragic events involving social proof in recent times occurred in the late 1970s when American cult leader Jim Jones steered his Peoples Temple church followers to move to a remote compound in the jungles of Guyana, South America, he named Jonestown. Later, complaints involving Jones' financial undertakings, coupled with allegations of human-rights abuses, resulted in congressional investigations of his activities. Jones, sensing collapse of his empire, planned for a mass suicide at Jonestown. He prepared a concoction of cyanide mixed with a grape-flavored drink mix, then convinced some of his most faithful followers to serve the deadly mixture to their children, and then consume it themselves. Sadly, most of the inhabitants were willing to drink the cyanide-laced concoction, even though they probably realized it would result in their own deaths. Since then, the expression, "Don't drink the Kool-Aid," has evolved into meaning, "Think for yourself," as opposed to following authority (or others), to the point you're sacrificing your own best interests.

Studies of social proof stress that the norm is most compelling when an individual is observing the behavior of another that is just like themselves. The conduct of those similar persons provides the best insights as to what constitutes correct behavior, or the right-thing-to-do.[xv]

Certainly, many prospects don't have a complete understanding of complex accounting, tax, and consulting issues, and how to resolve them. That is why having an excellent inventory of client case studies and testimonials can be so valuable in convincing prospects of your firm's capability to solve problems and add value. Following is a hypothetical case study used to describe data analytics transaction advisory.

XYZ LLP
Transaction Services Highlights
Facts

Acquisitions in the lower middle market are rife with challenges. Imperfect costing methods coupled with antiquated computer systems make buyers nervous about data being presented by the seller's investment bankers.

XYZ, LLP's transaction's team was engaged by a New York investment group to analyze the profitability of this Alabama-based highly-engineered component parts manufacturer that generated significant EBITDA margins. Target's products represented an integral part within each customer's end product, however, such component was not significant to customers' end product total cost. The buyer was concerned that the target's profitability was limited to select customers or a single product—creating a worrisome profit concentration. The seller was unable to provide the investment group with either customer or product line profitability as the accounting system didn't capture such information.

Issues

The investors were clearly intrigued by the company's earnings, however without a costing method or robust information system to alleviate their concerns, they would potentially need to forego the purchase opportunity.

Resolution

XYZ's professionals, in conjunction with the target entity's engineers clustered the products into eleven distinct groupings. Over the course of several days, the team was then able to create surrogate bills of materials and routings to determine approximate direct material and labor components for each of the product lines—and thus a product line contribution margin. This analysis ultimately concluded that for products manufactured in-house,

XYZ LLP (continued)

profitability within each of the product lines was fairly uniform—there was not an issue with either product or customer profitability concentration.

XYZ's team likewise learned that a meaningful level of the target's revenue (roughly 35%) came from either emergency orders or small lot batch requests—requiring additional engineering time or set-up costs. Notwithstanding the additional expenditures to produce such special orders, XYZ learned from various salesmen the target company didn't request upcharges or premium pricing.

XYZ finally was able to build an Excel bridge from the target company's accounting system that allowed the investor to monitor target product profitability up through the transaction closing date.

Why This Mattered

Our professionals were able to satisfy the buyer's key concern—that there was not problematic product line or customer profitability concentration. Moreover, discovery of the target's static pricing policies for small lot requests and rush orders highlighted a significant post-transaction pricing opportunity. Since the product was a relatively low-cost, but vital component to their customers' final products, meaningful pricing upcharges were possible for these "special orders." The buyer anticipated being able to boost EBITDA by $1-$2 million per year in the short-term, considerably improving their investment's return! Finally, the Excel bridge created as part of the transaction analysis, allowed the buyer to focus on other aspects of their 100-day plan, versus implementing a computer systems update immediately.

XYZ LLP Analysis of Product Line Profitability
Using Surrogate Bills of Materials and Routings
TTM Ending March 2015

Product line	A	B	C	D	E	F	G	H	I	J	K	Totals
Net sales revenue	2,764,000	2,088,000	900,000	1,448,000	24,000	700,000	2,116,000	140,000	544,000	244,000	48,000	11,016,000
Direct job costs	360,000	404,000	132,000	208,000	0	188,000	1,148,000	4,000	56,000	8,000	0	2,508,000
Throughput (material margin)	2,404,000	1,684,000	768,000	1,240,000	24,000	512,000	968,000	136,000	488,000	236,000	48,000	8,508,000
Percent	86.98%	80.65%	85.33%	85.64%	100.00%	73.14%	45.75%	97.14%	89.71%	96.72%	100.00%	77.23%
Variable manufacturing costs:												
Production labor (direct with fringes)	520,000	384,000	164,000	228,000	20,000	84,000	32,000	0	0	0	0	1,432,000
Manufacturing supplies and consumables	32,000	36,000	12,000	20,000	0	16,000	104,000	0	4,000	0	0	224,000
Total variable manufacturing costs	552,000	420,000	176,000	248,000	20,000	100,000	136,000	0	4,000	0	0	1,656,000
Contribution margin	1,852,000	1,264,000	592,000	992,000	4,000	412,000	832,000	136,000	484,000	236,000	48,000	6,852,000
Percent	67.0%	60.5%	65.8%	68.5%	16.7%	58.9%	39.3%	97.1%	89.0%	96.7%	100.0%	62.2%
Direct job costs by type:												
Purchases	216,000	316,000	96,000	88,000	0	0	1,144,000	4,000	56,000	8,000	0	1,928,000
Raw materials	144,000	88,000	36,000	120,000	0	188,000	4,000	0	0	0	0	580,000
Total direct job costs	360,000	404,000	132,000	208,000	0	188,000	1,148,000	4,000	56,000	8,000	0	2,508,000
Production labor by activity:												
Activity 1	124,000	44,000	8,000	24,000	0	0	32,000	0	0	0	0	232,000
Activity 2	0	0	0	0	0	0	0	0	0	0	0	0
Activity 3	48,000	44,000	8,000	24,000	0	80,000	0	0	0	0	0	204,000
Activity 4	8,000	12,000	4,000	4,000	0	0	0	0	0	0	0	28,000
Activity 5	152,000	88,000	64,000	92,000	16,000	4,000	0	0	0	0	0	416,000
Activity 6	44,000	36,000	24,000	28,000	0	0	0	0	0	0	0	132,000
Activity 7	92,000	112,000	32,000	28,000	4,000	0	0	0	0	0	0	268,000
Activity 8	52,000	48,000	24,000	28,000	0	0	0	0	0	0	0	152,000
Total production labor	520,000	384,000	164,000	228,000	20,000	84,000	32,000	0	0	0	0	1,432,000

XYZ LLP

Transaction Services Highlights

Note, case studies should be used to talk through an analogous problem or circumstance with your prospect, as opposed to being sent to them electronically or via mail to figure out on their own. They should be brief enough to get the key issue points across.

To the extent you are preparing case studies involving federal tax examples, you are *required* to obtain authorization from the client-taxpayer pursuant to IRC Section 7216, with harsh penalties for failure to comply. Certain states may have similar rules. See Appendix A for a sample authorization request form that is suitable for federal tax purposes. For nontax case studies, it obviously makes sense to obtain client consent as well to utilize their specific situation in any sales or marketing effort.

In addition to case studies, quantitatively demonstrating your dominance in a particular industry or niche, either nationally, or in your market, can also be an excellent social-proof technique. Further, references and referral calls from like clients to your prospect are great influencers under the social proof principle.

Now let's cover the fourth key social psychology influence law . . .

Liking

It shouldn't be earthshattering news to any of you that Cialdini's research shows that individuals have a greater tendency to say yes to the requests of those people they know and like. What is surprising, though, is that the concept of liking can be stretched in a multitude of ways by total strangers to get us to agree with their desires.[xvi] In this chapter section, we'll highlight issues impacting liking, and several ways to employ/improve use of this principle in CPA-related circles.

Physical attractiveness: Good-looking people have a clear leg-up in business and social interactions. What is shocking, though, is the halo effect attractiveness has on wide swath of other personality characteristics. Specifically, attractive people are deemed to be more talented, kind, honest, and intelligent by others, even though evaluators don't consciously realize they are making such judgments.[xvii] I'm sure many of you think it's really shallow for people to have sentiments about your CPA abilities based on your looks, but you'll have to deal with it, because they do.

Before you go out and make an appointment with a friendly plastic surgeon, we'll see that physical attractiveness encompasses a number of qualities, many controllable even if you weren't born with Hollywood hunk or vixen genes. According to Sylvia Ann Hewlett's research in her book *Executive Presence—The Missing Link Between Merit and Success*, the following are the top aspects of appearance according to senior leaders based on the gender of those being evaluated:[xviii]

Attribute	Women	Men
Being polished and groomed	35%	38%
Physically attractive, fit, slim	19%	16%
Simple, stylish clothes	12%	13%
Being tall	6%	16%
Being youthful and vigorous	6%	4%

The top-rated characteristic is under everyone's control, and the least manageable accounts for less than twenty percent, although fitness arguably can be impacted by many individuals. Augmenting Hewlett's conclusions are the following data point of interest:

• Although communications skills are a key attribute in assessing a person's competence, "No one even considers communication skills or thought leadership capabilities if your appearance telegraphs you as clueless. In other words, get this appearance thing wrong, and you're struck from the list."[xix]

• "Casual clothes may be the right choice for your firm's culture—but in their fit, brand and style, they should signify that you take your work—and those with whom you engage in it, very seriously. Poor grooming—including dirty or scuffed shoes, broken nails, runs in tights, etc.—compromises others' view of you, because you either don't notice your sloppiness or care enough to attend to it."[xx]

• "Achieving polish comes down to this golden rule: Minimize distractions from your skillsets and performance. Have professionals tend to your hair regularly. Invest in well-cut attire that complements your body type. Accessorize—but don't billboard your bling."[xxi]

Obviously this isn't a book about fashion, nevertheless, I'd be remise if I failed to note how many times I've witnessed clothing blunders that detracted from a professional's skills due to their dress or grooming in sales and marketing-related meetings. For example, professionals with shoes that looked like they refereed a mud-wrestling match the night before, or wearing attire that seemed as if they were showing off a bargain they copped at the Goodwill Store. In my view, if you're a partner-level CPA or rising star management member at your firm, you can, and should, budget several thousand dollars per year to regularly update your wardrobe to be sure you're looking your absolute best!

Similarity: As discussed in Chapter 2, when people are like each other, they tend to like each other. This includes factors like opinions, lifestyle, background, and personality traits. To the extent that these characteristics authentically exist in your encounters, feel free to avail them. You've also been exposed to multiple means to build rapport, which can help immensely in generating feelings of similarity.

Compliments: Probably not a huge surprise that we develop a shine towards those who are complimentary to us. What perhaps is noteworthy according to Cialdini is, "We are phenomenal suckers for flattery. Although there are limits to our gullibility—especially when we can be sure that the flatterer is trying to manipulate us—we tend, as a rule, to believe the praise and to like those who provide it, oftentimes when it is clearly false!"[xxii]

Hopefully, you've gleaned my view that you should be authentic in matters involving influence, persuasion, and sales. Genuinely complimenting those that have provided assistance to you on proposals, or congratulating those that have achieved remarkable successes in their business or industry can clearly be a smart approach under this guideline.

Contact and cooperation: Generally, people like things that are familiar to them. That's perhaps why, in certain instances, some prospects might only wish to work with a Big Four, or other nationally-recognized firms. The brands are familiar, making selection quicker because they are considered a safe choice. Nevertheless, this principle highlights that by proactively developing relationships with prospects, via meetings, calls, distributing substantive information, and the like, you can create that requisite acquaintance. Furthermore, with existing clients regularly acknowledging to client personnel that we are all working on the same team during lengthy projects, may be a way of building this cooperation link. In the tax arena, having tax professionals do tax return preparation in the field, something rarely done by most accounting firms, can be a great way to solidify your firm's relationships with more important clientele.

The liking standard involves many facets that are largely within our control . . . let's now turn our attention to the social psychology influencer known as . . .

Authority

According to Cialdini, "Information that is presented from a 'recognized authority' often provides a valuable shortcut to others on how to act."[xxiii] Of course, in today's data-overload society, getting that message through to prospects can sometimes be problematic. Certainly, being a real authority on a topic takes time. Nevertheless, there are ways to potentially shortcut the process, including:

- Leveraging off your firm's specialists who are experts in a niche needed by a client or prospect.

- Utilizing thought-leadership pieces and deliverables developed by your firm's top professionals that you study and present to the prospect.

- Authoring or co-authoring articles on relevant topics to clients or prospects, including drafting comment letters on proposed regulations on federal or state developments.

- Broadening your resume by proactively offering to speak at national, state, or local industry conferences.

- Updating clients or prospects with valuable insights from articles you've seen, regardless of the author, to demonstrate that you're on-your-game as it pertains to their industry or areas of importance to them.

Cialdini notes that looking the part of "an authority" also is vital, so being well dressed for each occasion as highlighted in the preceding section, is an essential ingredient.[xxiv]

Now let's overview the final social psychology area of influence . . .

Scarcity

According to Cialdini, "The idea of personal loss plays a large role in human decision making. In fact, people often seem more motivated by the thought of losing something, than the thought of gaining an item of equal value."[xxv] This phenomenon plays out with limited edition product offerings, when consumers don't want to miss out in owning that rare item of merchandise. Further, when restrictions are being imposed on us, let's say by the government, there is a natural push back from the citizens. Finally, when an item gets banned, people generally seem to want it even more, unless there is some real hazard linked to that particular thing being restricted.[xxvi]

The scarcity principle applies well beyond just stuff, and can come into play with messages, communications, and all types of intellectual information. The knowledge doesn't need to be somehow suppressed or restricted to be valuable to a potential recipient, just rare.[xxvii] In other words, where information isn't readily available elsewhere, it is deemed more influential to those it is conveyed. This can be particularly helpful to CPA firms that create innovative solutions, or that have devised know-how that their competitors lack.

Several years ago, my teammates within the SALT and public company tax co-sourcing practices utilized this scarcity principle to stoke both substantial annuity-type engagements and lucrative one-time consulting fees. During visits with one of our CPA firm alliance partners in Los Angeles, we learned of a tool created by a couple USC tax professors. Their software would identify a plethora of federal, state, and local income tax, sales and use tax and property tax credits, incentives, and savings opportunities—

real oddball tax benefits that were hard to detect. Basically, all you needed to have from a taxpayer were the addresses of their locations, and based on their zip codes, the software would list the tax breaks, and whether the savings were retroactive, allowing them to file a refund claim, or prospective, allowing them to take advantage of savings in the future by filing certain elections or other paperwork with a governmental agency.

We became one of a couple CPA firms in the U.S. to license the program, and then went to town visiting clients and prospects. Part of the team's pitch with prospects was the uniqueness of the GPS-based feature, with which we could capture buried tax savings that *no one else in our market was capable of*. This scarcity feature was incredibly attractive to just about everyone our co-sourcing professionals met with.

Our SALT practice later coupled an aspect of the liking principle with this software tool to produce some eye-popping tax savings and fees, by targeting sales calls within certain geographic areas of the U.S. where refundable credits seemed most opportune. One such sales and marketing initiative focused on rural parts of Louisiana, where the government was striving to jumpstart employment, and consequently had generous tax benefits for employers based in specific zip code locations. Since the SALT team was Midwest based, they hired a Louisiana-based CPA to accompany them on sales-related calls, combining the *similarity facet of liking* with the *scarcity* feature of the credit-finding software tool. The combination of the scarce GPS-based application, with a local CPA in the sales meetings had a powerful effect in attracting new work, even from businesses that thought they'd been-on-top-of the tax credit.

There may be other ways to ethically avail the scarcity influencer in our roles as CPAs, including:

- Advising a prospect about their need to make an engagement-acceptance decision to assure staffing is optimal.

- Emphasizing action on refund claims, elections, accounting method changes, and the like to beat statutory or regulatory deadlines.

- Stressing that a roundtable group you are forming has a limit on the number of attendees, and is based on a first-come basis.

By now, you've become indoctrinated to the power of these social aspects of influence, and have thought of even more ways to avail them in your firm. Thus far, we've concentrated on many topics that you can master as an individual to make a huge difference in both your interpersonal skills and persuasiveness. We'll now broaden the scope to include matters your firm, industry teams, or niche practice units should contemplate and resolve.

Chapter 3 References

[i]Cialdini, Ph.D., Robert B. *Influence—The Psychology of Persuasion*. William Morrow and Company, New, York, NY, 1993. Pages 2-3

[ii]Ibid. Pages 17-18

[iii]Ibid. Pages 18-21

[iv]Ibid. Page 30

[v]Ibid. Page 37

[vi]Ibid. Pages 42, 47

[vii]Vaynerchuk, Gary. *Crush It—Why NOW is the Time to Cash in on Your Passion*. HarperCollins Publishers, New York, NY, 2009.

[viii]Cialdini, Ph.D., Robert. *Instant Influence—How to Get What You Want in Any Business Situation*. Dartnell Audio, Chicago, IL, 1995.

[ix]Op. cit. Cialdini. *Influence—The Psychology of Persuasion.* Page 57

[x]Ibid. Page 67

[xi]Onesto, Li. *U.S. POWs during the Korean War.* Center for Global Research, globalresearch.org, September 3, 2008.

[ix]Op. cit. Cialdini. *Influence—The Psychology of Persuasion.* Page 116

[xiii]Ibid. Page 117

[xiv]Ibid. Page 129

[xv]Ibid. Pages 140-142

[xvi]Ibid. Page 167

[xvii]Ibid. Pages 171-172

[xviii]Hewlett, Sylvia Ann. *Executive Presence—The Missing Link Between Merit and Success.* HarperCollins Publishers, New York, NY, 2014. Page 82

[xix]Ibid. Page 81

[xx]Ibid. Page 86

[xxi]Ibid. Page 87

[xxii]Op. cit. Cialdini. *Influence—The Psychology of Persuasion.* Page 175

[xxiii]Ibid. Page 218

[xxiv]Ibid. Pages 227-229

[xxv]Ibid. Page 238

[xxvi]Ibid. Pages 251-253

[xvii]Ibid. Page 255

CHAPTER 4

THINGS YOUR FIRM, INDUSTRY TEAMS AND NICHE PRACTICE UNITS SHOULD ARTICULATE

As an individual, there is much you can do skill wise to help your firm's success in influence, persuasion, and sales settings. Nevertheless, as you go to market, having your team singing the same song is critically important in terms of what your firm does, its key differentiators from competitors, and why those differences matter to prospects, among other brand-related messages. Depending on your firm's scope of services and its degree of industry focus, the foregoing items may need to be tweaked slightly or individualized for the distinctions of each industry group or niche service. Ditto for those firms that tout its functional unit expertise, such as an exceptional tax practice, as a game-changer to prospects. We'll address these key areas for firms and their principal units to resolve in the pages that follow.

The Power of Anticipation

I've got to admit, I *really dislike* New England Patriots head coach Bill Belichick. I don't know him—never have met him. He's probably a great guy, but I loathe him nonetheless. His main atrocity is that he outcoaches and beats my beloved Indianapolis Colts seemingly every time they play. It hasn't mattered when or where the game took place, whether future Hall-of-Famer Peyton Manning was running the show, or if up-and-comer Andrew Luck was under center. The result always has been pretty much the same—a loss.

In what is probably my all-time favorite sports book, David Halberstan's *The Education of a Coach*, the author distills many of the reasons Belichick's won four Super Bowls, and been to two others as the Pats' head coach.[i] When you absorb this biography, you see an image of guy that is scary smart, disciplined as the day is long, and a tireless worker. What probably sets him apart, though, is his ability to break down an opponent's films and craft a game plan based on his predictions of what an opponent is likely to do. In the 2001 Super Bowl, for example, Belichick created a scheme to shutdown prolific St. Louis Rams' running back Marshall Faulk by chipping him every single play he was on the field, rendering him inconsequential in the game. Coach Belichick felt that Faulk would lose his mojo by the second half with his defense's nonstop hits, even when Marshall didn't have the ball. Eleven years later, Faulk was still so frustrated with the Rams' performance and his rushing stats that game, he said, "The Patriots seemed to be so perfectly prepared for them, that they must have used espionage."[ii]

On December 26, 2004, 10-year old Tilly Smith was vacationing at Mai Khao Beach on Phuket Island, Thailand, when she saw something odd, the ocean recede. The girl told her parents, who passed a cautionary note on to others. Because of Tilly's insight, the beach was completely evacuated by the time a tsunami hit the shoreline, a result of the 9.3 magnitude Sumatra—Andaman quake, one of the most powerful earthquakes ever recorded. Mai Khao Beach was one of the few beaches on Phuket Island that sustained no casualties from the tsunami, a series of tidal waves that claimed more than 230,000 people in 14 countries that day.[iii]

"Tilly had learned in her geography class back in England a few weeks before, that one telltale sign of a tsunami is a sudden pulling back of the water's edge—the ocean's version of sucking in a breath, before exhaling with an exploding blast of destruction. In other areas of Southeast Asia, children saw this receding ocean— and saw it as a chance to go onto freshly exposed stretches of beach to collect shells. Tragically, nobody knew to tell them any different."[iv]

————

In 2006, John Paulson was a relatively unknown hedge fund manager that engaged mainly in trades focused on corporate takeovers and mergers. Observing at the time that there was mass hysteria involving U.S. housing, home equity loans and subprime credit—and what seemed to be extremely poor underwriting standards on these loans, Paulson organized a fund, the Paulson Credit Opportunity Fund (PCOF) to bet against subprime mortgages using an insurance-like device called credit default swaps (CDSs). In Paulson's investment thesis, the CDSs would become significantly more valuable to the extent the worth of the subprime mortgages declined.

Paulson's PCOF purchased most of the CDS protection on the riskiest slice of securities because he predicted that even if housing had a minor correction, their value would be severely impaired or perhaps, totally wiped out. As we all know, housing and subprime mortgages sustained a massive correction in 2007, and the PCOF and Paulson profited handsomely. How handsomely? Paulson's 2007 paycheck was reported to be in the $4 billion range.

So, what do Belichick, Smith and Paulson's stories have in common? They **all** highlight the compelling power of anticipation: Being able to predict an occurrence, and then planning and preparing accordingly. Thankfully, events like the Super Bowl aren't riding on your CPA team's anticipation skills. However, your firm's influence, persuasion, and sales-related successes can skyrocket to the extent you properly think-through and practice answers to those questions the marketplace surely wants to know about. Not the, "blah, blah, blah," about how good you are service wise—rather, answers to important questions such as:

- What business problems do you *really* solve?

- Prospects have turned to your firm as a whole, your industry team, functional unit, or niche practices when they are frustrated about _____?

- What makes your firm or industry team different from your competition?

- What difference does your difference(s) make in terms of risk, time, and money?

- If you were sitting in your prospect's chair right now, what are the *biggest* issues or concerns in terms of engaging your firm?"

- How are your firm's professionals able to mitigate those issues and/or concerns?[v]

These are not easy questions to answer when you really think about it. Those firms and teams that go through this thought exercise however, can dramatically sharpen their marketplace distinctions, and be able to reply effectively to prospects, versus competitor firms that fail to anticipate.

Let's explore these questions a bit further—and how an accounting or advisory firm might approach answering these inquiries.

What Business Problems Do You Really Solve?[vi]

Identifying the business challenges your firm actually addresses can be a great starting point in setting the stage for what distinguishes your firm from competitors in the market. This question may make sense to answer for the firm overall, principal industry teams, and other niche practices, too. For example, a firm in general might approach responding to this question as follows:

The business problems our firm solve for clients like you include:

- Compliance, and the accurate need for it.

- Helping to keep integrity within your business.

- Assisting your team in understanding industry rules and regulations, and how to practically implement them.

- Providing clarity about how to expand into multi-state and global markets.

- Financial decision-making, especially when the answers aren't readily apparent.

A niche practice, similar to the data-analytics-based transaction services group I was recently involved with, conceivably would stress the following points:

The business problems our transactions practice solve for financial buyers like you include:

- Ameliorating risks in purchasing illiquid privately-owned businesses.

- Creating transparency about the businesses a PE firm targets, including customer profitability, profit density, and murky threats such as functionally obsolete inventories.

- Identifying other levers of profitability, and which ones to pull to fuel post-transaction profitability.

It's your turn to be creative, so in the space below, articulate what business-related problems your firm or industry team *really* solve:

_____

_____

_____

_____

_____

_____

_____

_____

_____

_____

_____

_____

_____

Prospects Have Turned to Our Firm When They Are Frustrated About: _____?[vii]

The focus of this question is that it highlights the common business problems prospects (who became your clients), have had with the CPA industry, or with a specific type of accounting firm competitor. For example, if your firm is a middle-market advisory house, crafting answers for businesses that are moving down-market from a national or Big Four advisor, and up-market from a local or small regional firm likely makes sense.

For down-market buyers, the mid-market firm might say something like the following:

Smaller-cap public companies have turned to our firm, when they are frustrated about:

- Access and responsiveness: The lack of accessibility to their (audit/tax/other) partner because they are mainly focused on _____ (name a couple large public companies in your market).

- Resources: Although the big boy firms have all the talent in the world to solve problems, these talented people aren't located anywhere near our city.

- The school bus syndrome: Every year when the audit kicks off, it looks like they're emptying out a school bus full of kids in front of your office to work on the engagement.

- Fees versus value: Getting a one-thousand-dollar bill for every thirty-minute call, on top of paying for all that big-firm overhead for the audit and tax compliance work.

You get the picture.

For potential up-market buyers, the response might be as follows:

Growing privately-held companies have turned to our firm when they are frustrated about:

- **Resources:** Many growing businesses have had a great personal relationship with their CPA firm's partners, and they are terrific guys, *but* they unwittingly cause huge tax risks and exposures due to their limited in-house SALT and international talent.

- **Specialization:** We've seen many manufacturing companies like yours move our way because their CPA firm's partner has to cover a lot of different industries, and can't possibly be up-to-speed on all of them.

By the way, the foregoing points aren't intended to pick on big or small firms, you can craft compelling answers to this question no matter what type of firm yours is. It all comes down to thinking about where your opportunities come from, or where you want them to start coming from, and crafting creative, thoughtful responses.

Okay, let's get to work and answer the question for your firm, industry team, etc.:

_____

_____

_____

_____

_____

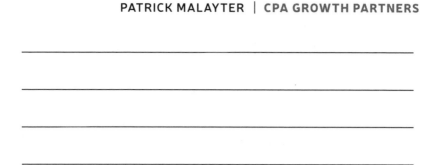

What Makes You Different From Your Competition?[viii]

Let's face it, many prospective clients don't shop for new CPAs, or for that matter, any professional services firms on a day-in, day-out basis. After being in the business for more than thirty-five years, my sense is that within a certain strata of accounting-advisory firm, they all pretty much look the same to a potential buyer. The Big Four look alike, national firms are pretty similar, the super-regionals match-up well, and local shops often seem to look and feel the same. A fairly astute question you might receive is, "What *does* make you different?" Even if you aren't asked, wouldn't it be helpful to be able to articulate your differences at an appropriate time?

A real benefit of this exercise is to be able to educate an otherwise incisive buyer, which can be invaluable in de-commoditizing services that might, at first blush, look the same.

Thinking about my most recent years in public accounting, coupled with the industry groups I spent the most time with, here's how I would articulate what made my teammates different from competitors:

- Our partners are truly invested in client engagements, they don't make cameo appearances during the course of an audit.

- We have a six-to-one staff/partner leverage ratio, many of our like competitors have staff-to-partner ratios double that.

• As a firm, we are incredibly disciplined operationally, in client acceptance matters, risk management, and with respect to centralized engagement and transaction reviews.

On their own, the statement might not seem all that eye-popping, that's why you'll need to continue through *all the exercises* in this chapter. Now it's your turn. In the space below, articulate what makes your firm or industry team different from your competitors:

_____

_____

_____

_____

_____

_____

_____

_____

_____

_____

_____

_____

_____

What Difference Does Your Difference(s) Make in Terms of Risk, Time and Money?[ix]

The real magic from the preceding section arises from *why does this matter* to the prospective client. Staff ratios, having partners working in-the-field, your firm's discipline, are throwaway points until you can describe what it means to *them*, in terms of risks, time, and money.

Building on the previous question's responses, the following could be some of the differences that the above-noted differentiators might make to a prospect:

- With our partners *being onsite* during your engagement, we are *gaining greater insight* about ways to improve your operations, and solving problematic job-related issues quicker.

- Our professionals are substantially better supervised as a result of the degree of partner involvement. Your financial executives aren't wasting time with greenhorn staff CPA questions.

- The collaborative centralized review process helps avoid unexpected surprises and report issuance delays that some other firms are infamous for, helping assure you don't miss key deadlines with banks and other interested parties.

- The risk management processes we use result in a much more competitive cost structure, which clients frequently see fee-wise compared to larger firm advisors.

All right, with those points serving as a model, what are the differences your firm or industry team distinguishing factors mean to a prospect in terms of risk, time or money?

_____

_____

_____

_____

_____

_____

_____

_____

_____

_____

_____

Remember, like most exercises, the effort your team and you put forth in thinking through genuine differentiators, and why they matter, can have a persuasive marketplace impact. You clearly want to avoid taking a perfunctory approach by putting your team's full brainpower to work.

If You Were Sitting in Your Prospect's Chair Right Now, What Are the Biggest Issues or Concerns in Terms of Engaging Your Firm?[x]

The process of anticipation also includes preparing in advance for other possibilities, such as reasons that might delay a prospect from engaging your firm. There are a variety of fears, limitations and other causes that can get in the way of your team receiving an opportunity to serve a prospect that truly needs to make a change, and deserves better. Through the years I've observed that people make decisions for their own reasons, not yours. Consequently, each prospective client's reservations need to be individually determined, so you can potentially help them overcome their resistance to change. Here are some of the various issues or concerns I've heard or otherwise perceived through the years:

- Change is scary—the devil you know is sometimes better than the one you don't know.

- Trust—how do we know you guys are for real?

- The CFO or other key employee may lose his or her protector, the incumbent advisor.

- If we make a change to your firm, and it goes poorly, it can be a career breaker.

- Will we have the time to deal with this?

- How do we let go of a friend, a CPA we've had a relationship with for years?

- How will we handle the transition?

- Will this change in firms end up costing us even more?

- The existing financial staff may lose their scapegoat.

- How will our bankers, or other outsiders view this?

Take a few moments now to augment the foregoing list with your real life list of issues or concerns that a prospect might have in engaging your firm, industry team, or practice niche:

_____

_____

_____

_____

_____

_____

_____

_____

_____

_____

How Are Your Firm's Professionals Able to Mitigate Those Issues and/or Concerns?

In Richard Bandler and John LaValle's 1996 book, *Persuasion Engineering*, the authors note that to the extent you can *anticipate* what a prospect's issues and/or concerns are going to be, you can "inoculate" such concerns, and lessen the chances of them being raised (i.e., as an objection).[xi] How? By weaving in the potential concerns as part of your normal prospect conversation, and noting how they've been effectively resolved by your firm.

Here is an example. During the late 1990s our firm initiated a research and experimentation tax credit practice (the R&E credit practice), largely for manufacturing-related clientele and targets. A more lucrative credit was generally earned by taxpayers via increasing research-related expenditures over a base period, for most companies the years being 1984 to 1988. There were a number of inherent complications for mid-market companies that wanted to claim the credit—because they didn't normally track specific research projects, keep records of who worked on projects, or have contemporaneous documents going back to the base period years. Prospective clients often expressed concern about how much time their personnel would spend on this type of engagement, and worried about the cost/benefit to their company.

After fumbling-through several prospect meetings, the team learned what a typical client's concerns were, and subsequently incorporated such matters as part of each prospect meeting, and how they were easily resolved. Once the team could anticipate the prospect's issues, and address them in conversations, the number of engagements skyrocketed.

There are several other ways to address issues or concerns head-on, besides incorporating inoculation into your prospect sessions, including:

- Creating case studies surrounding the types of challenges prospects face, and how your firm can resolve them (see Chapter 3's discussion on social proof).

- For areas such as client transitioning from the predecessor CPA firm to your shop, crafting a simple one-page handout that shows how the onboarding process is handled.

- Having a recently-converted client proactively call your prospect with a short message about how efficient and painless transition was, or describe how you satisfactorily handled their type of engagement previously.

Now let's rev-up your anticipation skills by taking the four most prominent issues and concerns prospects are likely to have from the preceding section, and list out specifically how your firm or industry team can proactively address or inoculate them:

Issue/concern # 1:

_____

_____

_____

_____

_____

_____

Ways to address/inoculate:

_____

_____

_____

_____

_____

_____

_____

Issue/concern # 2:

_____

_____

_____

_____

_____

Ways to address/inoculate:

_____

_____

_____

_____

_____

Issue/concern # 3:

_____

_____

_____

_____

_____

_____

Ways to address/inoculate:

_____

_____

_____

_____

_____

_____

Issue/concern # 4:

_____

_____

_____

_____

_____

_____

_____

Ways to address/inoculate:

_____

_____

_____

_____

_____

_____

_____

This chapter has focused on anticipating questions the marketplace will conceivably ask of your firm and industry teams. Thoughtfully engaging in the above exercises can produce _outstanding_ differentiators and drive consistent market messages—helping your firm win even more.

Chapter 5 reveals a collective strategy to engage _all your firm's professionals_ in practice expansion, an approach called the E^4 Growth Method.

Chapter 4 References

[i]Halberstam, David. *The Education of a Coach*. Hyperion Books, New York, NY, 2005.

[ii]Smith, Michael David. Marshall Faulk: *Patriots Cheated the Rams Out of a Super Bowl*. Profootballtalk.nbccports.com, January 30, 2013.

[iii]Burrus, Daniel—with Mann, John David. *Flash Foresight—How to See the Invisible and Do the Impossible*. HarperCollins Publishers, New York, NY, 2011. Pages 40-41

[iv]Ibid. Page 41

[v]McNaughton, Gene. *The Psychology and Strategy of Consultative Selling with Major Accounts*. Elite Concepts, Inc. San Diego, CA, 2009. Pages 3-5

[vi]Ibid.

[vii]Ibid.

[viii]Ibid.

[ix]Ibid.

[x]Ibid.

[xi]Bandler, Richard and LaValle John. *Persuasion Engineering*. Meta Publications, Capitola, CA 1996. Pages 195-196

CHAPTER 5

THERE IS A ROLE FOR EVERYONE: AVAILING THE E⁴ GROWTH METHOD

As discussed in Chapter 1, there is a vast *difference* between the organic growth rates of top-quartile growing CPA firms and those in the bottom fourth, so much so, that those top firms will lap their peer firms that are pulling up the rear in the next five years, should those trends continue. Of course, the whole point of this book is that your firm's historic unsatisfactory practice expansion scorecard need not be its future way of life. Results *can*, and *will* change for the good, with better decisions, training, resolve, strategy, and leadership from the very top of your organization.

The Seven Ways to Grow Your Firm's Top Line

Perhaps you, the reader, will point out oversights in my line of thinking, but from where I sit, there are seven potential ways your firm can grow the overall top line. Following is a concise synopsis of each, along with commentary:

CPA Firm Mergers

No doubt, an effective means to bolster a firm's revenues, resources, and presence can involve a merger. Several top CPA firms have increased their prominence both nationally or in key markets via strategic unions—including the Dixon Hughes

Goodman, CliftonLarsonAllen, and CohenReznick fusions, along with Blackman Kallick's merger into Plante Moran. Of course, those noted firms had, and continue to have, plenty of talent internally to find, successfully negotiate, and properly integrate deals.

Certainly, many M&A transactions have occurred involving local and regional firms in the recent past as well, although the internal executive bandwidth at such shops often isn't quite as wide. Talking with those familiar with some of these transactions, the combined firm may practice under one firm name, but the merger partners frequently practice pretty much as they did pre-merge. As the private equity world will confirm, an ill-conceived or poorly integrated merger can leave the combined unit in worse shape than the firms were beforehand.

Having lived through several mergers personally, there is a unique phenomenon that occurs with the acquired firm. Clients have an excuse to reevaluate their professional services arrangement as a result of the change, and a subset often go out for proposal, even when their engagement team stays in place. Couple that with your strongest CPA firm competition egging the process on by whispering in your clients' ears about how bad their service will be due to the merger. It's not all sunshine and lollypops for either of the merger partners.

In short, there are compelling reasons to engage in merger transactions from a scale standpoint, and they are a sure-fire way to grow, but multiple risks should be addressed as well.

Product and Service Innovation

Many years ago, the late Peter Drucker—the father of business consulting, made an observation that has been lost in the sands of time. He wrote, "Because the purpose of business is to create a customer, the business enterprise has two, and only two basic functions: marketing and innovation. Marketing and innovation produce results; all the rest are costs."[i]

You might be thinking, whoa there is a *lot* more to business than just that—like providing excellent client service, or that a new customer will soon go bye-bye. I'd agree with you 100 percent. We'd all probably concur however, that innovation *is* a critically needed and desired business ability.

A handful of accounting firms, most notably Crowe Horwath, embrace the importance of product and service innovation. As part of its commitment to this, Crowe named Derek Bang, a partner, as its first chief innovation officer in October 2013, responsible for leading the New Product Development Team. Two of the products created in the healthcare revenue cycle and nonprofit tax software arenas generated more than $100 million in revenue, Crowe recently reported, which partially explains the firm's robust growth.[ii] Having spoken with several CPA firm competitors of Crowe, these new products have had a disruptive impact, dislodging several of their longstanding client relationships.

Many professional services firms struggle with incubating new services, practices, tools, and other initiatives. However, successful innovating is simply rooted in basic strategy, followed by leadership's and the innovation team's action, execution, and perseverance. Unfortunately, taking partners or other talented high-level professionals offline to engage in these development-related activities is viewed as too costly by many firms.

Market or Inflation-related Fee Increases

Certainly since the Great Recession, many clients have pushed back on accounting-related fee increases, reflecting the pricing tension they've had with their own customers. Notwithstanding the challenges, *The Journal of Accountancy* recently reported that audit fee increases in 2013 for public companies averaged 4.5 percent, whereas private businesses incurred a 3.7-percent bump in audit-related fees. The survey likewise stated nonprofits paid on average 1.5 percent more in attest fees in 2013. Public companies generally attributed the fee increases to reviews of manual controls and other PCAOB-related items, whereas the private entities and nonprofits said inflation was the cause for the fee hikes.[iii]

Obviously, your firm's ability to pass-along market or inflation-related fee bumps depends on a number of factors, including your competition, the industries you're serving, and other market conditions in your locale. The article simply highlights CPA firms are capturing fee increases, and perhaps your firm can too.

Availing the E⁴ Growth Method

The E⁴ Growth Method involves your firm's conjunctive focus on:

Essential clients: These are the anchor clients of your firm or office, the ones that you're going to shed some real tears over if they depart. They are also the same clients your most hated competitors are plotting right now to steal from you, or get a share of their professional services spends. Having set plans to assure these are the greatest raving fans of your firm are crucial. Client losses happen in the course of business, you can't let these be among them.

Expansion clients: Most partners in your firm likely have a half-dozen or so expansion clients. These are excellent clients that, for whatever reason, are not availing one-or-more of the valuable services your firm provides. Oftentimes, the reason can be a partner's gatekeeper tendencies, or busyness. Identifying opportunities by office industry teams or functional specialists can be a way of rooting out prospects. Note: expansion clients are not mutually exclusive of essential clients, in fact, there are often many low-hanging-fruit opportunities within the essential client category at your firm.

Emerging issues: These are regulatory agency changes or accounting body rule modifications that apply to a broad segment of clients. These types of changes occur almost every year or two in the CPA industry. A current example is the Treasury Department's repair regulations finalized in 2013. Most firms fail to approach implementation of these emerging issue developments in a strategic, cohesive manner, often losing out on a collective multi-million dollar fee opportunity, while simultaneously exposing the firm to malpractice risks (due to spotty adoptions within the client base).

External client opportunities: This is self-explanatory in terms of what it is, and the methodology for expanding revenues with these opportunities will be discussed further below, and in subsequent chapters of this book.

With this background, let's delve into the first aspect of Availing the E^4 Growth Method.

Essential Clients

As noted above, essential clients are those anchor clients of your office or firm. Some firms might define these clients via the 80/20-rule, others, by some other percentage of clients generating a significant amount of fees/profits. Certainly most of us intuitively know it's far more expensive to obtain a new client versus keep existing clientele. What so few CPA firms truly appreciate is just *how* important retaining these important clientele can be to the long-term growth and profitability of their firm. This section will share various data points on retention, how critical it is to your practice expansion strategy, as well as means to foster essential client stickiness.

Perhaps the nation's principal thought leader on the significance of customer retention, as measured by loyalty is Bain & Company Partner and founder of its Loyalty Practice, Frederick Reichheld. In his seminal book, *The Loyalty Effect—The Hidden Force Behind Growth, Profits and Lasting Value,* Reichheld states, "Relative retention explains profits better than market share, scale, cost position or any other variable usually associated with competitive advantage."[iv] Under this notion, loyalty involves providing so much value to customers, that there are oceans of left-over funds available for employees and owners.

Client loyalty and retention have some basic arithmetic components. Using the Rule of 72's effect, a CPA firm that has a five percentage point better client retention rate than its similarly-sized competitor will grow to twice the size of the competitor over fourteen years, based solely on retention. Reichheld postulates though, that, "Raising client retention by five percentage points may conceivably increase the value of an average customer by 25 to 100 percent. Further, the consequences of customer retention compound over time, so that even tiny changes can have a cascading effect on fees and profits."[v] In the graph below, retention has an exponential impact on desirable factors such as:

- Base profits

- Per customer revenue growth

- Operating costs

- Referral potential

- Premium pricing

The Impact of Retention, and its Effect on Profitability Components[vi]

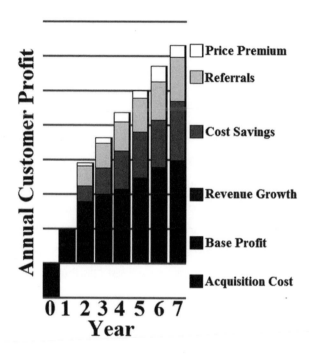

Client acquisition costs: In most CPA firms, client acquisition costs include a portion of your marketing team's work on new client efforts, along with administrative time related to proposal preparation. Since most new client proposals are driven by partners, directors, and other management professionals, their time costs are part of the overall acquisition cost charge.[vii]

Base profit: This is a fairly straightforward concept in terms of what it constitutes, and obviously, the longer the client is in your firm's house, the longer you'll enjoy these base profits.[viii]

Revenue growth: With more sophisticated clients, their businesses normally gain size and complexity through time, and typically command greater fees as a result. Further, as clients extend their tenure with your firm, they usually are purchasers of additional services, or at least are amenable to your providing additional services.[ix]

Cost savings: Recurring clientele have implicit cost savings built in. Their data is loaded within your firm's electronic filing systems so that annual set-up is speedy and efficient. There is likely continuity of engagement partners, and potentially stability in managers and some staff from the preceding year, minimizing learning time related to the company.[x]

Referrals: Although many CPA firms do not capitalize on the referral value of loyal, well-satisfied existing clientele, many other industries master ways to capture this byproduct of service excellence. Reichheld's research finds that prospects introduced to your firm via referral from an existing client tend to be more profitable and have longer longevity versus clients you've gained via an RFP.[xi]

Price premium: Longstanding clientele generally have less price sensitivity, especially for add-on services. Considering the degree of cutthroat pricing occurring on many audit- and tax-related RFPs, mature clients for all intents and purposes pay greater fees for the same type of work than new clients. This can be somewhat problematic if one of these regulars, for whatever reason, has an account review and goes-out-for-bid.[xii]

So retention and loyalty matter, what's sobering is how tenuous many client relationships are.

How Loyal are Your Essential Clients?

Indianapolis-based Walker Research, Inc., is an entity engaged in the customer intelligence business. Walker assists companies so they become more astute about their customers, by surveying them on their degree of satisfaction with their provider, as well as anticipating customers' future interactions and spending with their provider. Walker utilizes predictive analytics and other approaches in arriving at its conclusions. Based on Walker's body of work for market-leading companies that are engaged in business-to-business commerce, they've derived the following chart that highlights four classes that customers or clients typically fall:

Accessible	**Truly Loyal**
High Risk	**Trapped**

Let's briefly review what the quadrants mean—and the potential impact on client retention:

Truly loyal: This is the type of client that most CPA firms love having, and want even more of. They are partners, who value your services, repelling competitors that call on them, and spending larger amounts with your firm than do other clientele. These are the clientele that truly enhance your firm's profitability. The problem is that they typically represent only half of clients.[xiii]

Trapped: These are existing clients that need your services, that are using your services because they have to, but might not be using you a year from now. Their fees might look secure and profitable to you now, but they might or might not be around if something doesn't change, for the good, in terms of your relationship. These clients often are more difficult to service, and are often not utilizing the breadth of services your firm offers. Incredibly, the trapped quadrant at most companies represent 15 to 25 percent of clientele per Walker's statistics. The good news is that these clients have the potential to be brought into the fold of truly loyal clients.[xiv]

High Risk: These are clients that are unhappy and will be gone soon, assuming there isn't relatively rapid action taken to repair aspects of the relationship. Per Walker's analysis, clients in this quadrant represent 15 to 20 percent of revenue, obviously a huge revenue risk. Turning these clients around requires some proactive changes to the way you're relating to them, in terms of your personnel, attention or services.[xv]

Accessible: Walker believes this quadrant of client constitutes only about 5 percent of revenues. They *love* your firm, but at some point in the future, won't need your services anymore. They may have been acquired by a private equity firm, for example, and might be required to use another provider sometime in the future.[xvi]

In addition to the retention aspects of Walker's loyalty matrix, their studies also note differing levels of marginal profitability of clientele as follows:

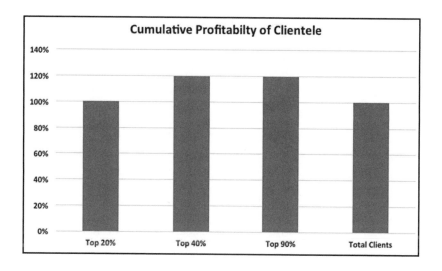

Walker finds that at most businesses, the top 20 percent of clientele generates 100 percent of their firm's overall profitability. The second fifth adds an additional 20 percent to profitability. Incredibly, Walker's research indicates the next 50 percent of clientele have no net improvement to profitability whatsoever, and the final 10 percent actually have a *diminishing effect* on profits of 20 percent due to their high service costs.[xvii]

The challenge for most firms is to find ways to either jettison or improve means to deliver services to that bottom 10 percent of clients, along with advancing the profitability of the non-accretive 50 percent. Walker's work above involves a variety of B-to-B entities, and obviously may differ from your shop's experiences.

In our industry specifically, recent surveys and research of accounting firm clientele by CCH reveals that clients measure loyalty much more by the "what have you done for me lately yardstick." Among the key findings in their study involving CPA firm client retention, are:

- "Retention risks are real for CPA firms. Not only are clients being prospected by other accounting firms, a meaningful number are actually contemplating a change in advisor.

- "The top service area of concern for both business and individual clients involves minimizing taxes. Seventy-three percent of businesses stated minimizing taxes were of prime concern (the number-two issue for companies involved federal, state, and local tax compliance). Sixty-nine percent of individuals rated minimizing tax liabilities as number one.

- "Forty-seven percent of business clients garnered the greatest value from their CPA firm relationship via their partner, while another 42 percent derived their most significant value from non-partner CPAs at the firm. Team contact and relationships matter!

- "Gaps exist between client expectations for performance on key criteria and the firm's performance on delivering (see discussion below).

- "While 79 percent of business clients say they are generally satisfied with their CPA firm, of that group, only 17 percent say they are *completely* satisfied. Surveyed business clients further indicated that 15 percent were 'very likely' to change accounting firms, and another 21 percent stated they were 'somewhat likely' to change firms. This data correlates somewhat with Walker's figures related to trapped and high risk clients.

- "Most clients won't tell you they are dissatisfied unless you ask them, they'll just stop doing business with you.

- "The top reason clients consider leaving their existing firm is because the firm does not regularly check with them on their changing needs."[xviii]

Another data point from the CCH survey worthy of review involves gaps between important issues when choosing a CPA firm, versus business clients' perceptions of actual performance by their current CPAs. Following are the greatest variances in the clients' eye:[xix]

Issue	Importance Rating	Performance Rating
Helps lower our taxes	81%	70%
Provides right tools to their staff	81%	70%
Specializes in services we need	82%	72%
Informs us of regulations affecting us	83%	74%
Informs us about changing regulations	84%	75%

Furthermore, a Bay Street Group, LLC, study involving why clients fire their accountant, versus the CPA's perception as to why it happened, found that roughly 66 percent of clients that dismissed their CPA said they did so due to poor client service and inattentiveness. Only 27 percent of CPAs attributed the client leaving to their service-related shortcomings.[xx]

Now that we've properly emphasized how *critical* essential clients can be to your CPA firm's growth and profitability, just how vulnerable your key clientele may be, and what clients are saying is important to them, let's learn how to keep them.

Strategies to Retain Essential Clients

Let's summarize a handful of our key learnings thus far:

1. Client loyalty and retention have a meaningful role in growth and profitability, and small positive changes can have a significant long-term impact.

2. The top 40 percent of clients are generating your shop's profits. The bottom 60 percent are theoretically non-accretive or possibly reducing profitability.

3. There is a considerable percentage of clients who are receptive to another CPA firm's marketing and sales calls, and are at risk.

4. With a few exceptions (e.g., governmental entities and certain nonprofit organizations), clients have keen interest in tax-related compliance issues and in your firm minimizing their taxes.

5. Clients typically enjoy interacting with their CPA firm's partners and non-partner CPA professionals.

6. You are most likely to be terminated by clients for poor service and inattentiveness. They will *consider leaving* to the extent you do not regularly check-in with them on their changing needs.

7. Clients will tell you they aren't happy, but only if you ask.

Here's the great news. If you became a CPA to work with and help clients, and are engaged with their business-related challenges, there is an *incredibly* important role for you in serving your firm's essential clients well. There's no need for you to be flashy, *you just need to have passion to deliver great client service.*

What your office's or firm's leadership needs, though, is to have an essential client strategy, execution skills, and some backbone to deal with inevitable noncompliance and blowback. Step one involves figuring out who these essential clients are by using the 80/20 rule or some other manageable percentage (to determine which clients are generating a significant amount of fees and profits). Some flexibility is in order to include clients who may not be a high-fee or profit patrons yet, but carry some other prominence. Sure, you want to take good care of all clients, but you *really* want to take *exceptional* care of your firm's essential clients.

How do you do that? Although I'm sure you'll augment this list based on the uniqueness of your practice, here are several ways to potentially make their relationship extraordinary:

- To the extent the client is a business-audit client, be sure there is a "dual-service partner team" serving the account (e.g. an audit and tax partner). Be sure that billing responsibilities are bifurcated so that each professional has that feeling of accountability to the client. This can eventually be beneficial for your firm's succession strategy as well.

- Assure that these clients are first-to-be-scheduled.

- Find means of regularly communicating with them about regulatory updates and the like. If they're in a specific industry, for example, as pronouncements arise affecting their business, they're on your speed-dial.

- Consider having partners and engagement management setting up Google Alerts for both the essential client company and its key individuals. When a development occurs, you'll be able to respond with a congratulatory email or an inquiry.

- Since tax is important to a huge number of these clients, and many of these folks like interacting with their CPA firm's professionals, schedule the tax return preparation to be done at the client's place of business. Being onsite leads to better insight about the client and its people.

- Have tax returns completed and delivered within a comfortable timeframe before the due dates. It is unbelievable how many high-profile calendar-year corporate taxpayer returns are issued late in the game, even on September 14th!

- For essential business clients and key individuals, deliver the tax returns in person.

- Consider issuing a "tax opportunity letter" for delivery shortly after the tax return's completion. The letter can include tax savings opportunities for the client to consider now or in the near term, and legislation or regulatory changes they need to be aware of. Clients absolutely *love* this focus on what are often their most significant business and personal monetary concerns.

- If you've done unique things to help save the client money, avoid risk, or something similar, consider drafting a case study with the client's approval.

- Have a face-to-face debrief session with the client once an engagement is complete. What went well? What can we improve upon? How can we do an even better job serving you in the future?

- Consider periodic formal client surveys given to essential clients from an independent organization to obtain unbiased perspectives on your firm's relationships.

What about those clients that aren't the essential clients? We don't advocate jettisoning clients, unless they develop ethical issues, are mean-spirited with your staff, or don't pay their bills. We fully believe in staffing appropriately and leveraging professionals based on the complexity and sophistication of a client. There are only so many hours in a day, and your best and brightest need to be laser-focused on your most valuable customers, the essential clients.

Expansion Clients

These are already first-rate clients at your firm, who for whatever reason, are not taking advantage of one-or-more of the services your shop provides. They can include clientele where they have a potential planning idea that can either save them money or time, or reduce risk at the client's business. As described previously, expansion clients are not mutually-exclusive from the essential clients group, in fact, there are often many service expansion opportunities within the essential client category.

What is great about expansion clients is that they are already existing patrons of your firm, and perhaps the easiest group to introduce and sell new services. As described in this book's Preface, many years ago as a manager and senior manager, developing expansion clients was how I cut-my-teeth on sales and marketing activities. If you think about the CCH survey, and what clients want from their advisor, they want proactive advice, not just a number cruncher. This is a role every manager, senior manager, director, and partner can partake in to build their firm's top-line. It's just part of providing excellent service. Who among us can argue against that?

What gets in the way of CPAs taking action to expand services to existing clients? Often, the reason can be a partner's gatekeeper tendencies—they don't want others in the firm to threaten their client relationship. Other times, it's the partner's busyness—they simply don't want to take on more work. Occasionally, the CPA has limiting beliefs, and is engaging in a mind-reading exercise, claiming they *already know how the client will react* to the introduction of a new service. However, what I've seen most times is a *fearful partner*, fearful that the client will ask *why* the partner hadn't mentioned the service already. As if the client cares much about your personal insecurities or embarrassment.

As a professional who created or co-developed multiple practices from scratch, clients rarely ask *"the why question."* But, when *another CPA firm* contacts them about an idea you've failed to address, well, it can get pretty ugly for you.

I heard about one of those dreadful encounters between a leading CPA firm and one of their prominent clients several years ago from a friend who was the national tax director at that particular accounting firm. Apparently, one of the Big Four firms had organized a tax accounting methods hit-squad to call on large manufacturing companies in the southeastern U.S. Their client, thirsty for tax savings, agreed to let the Big Four firm inspect previously filed tax returns for opportunities. The hit-squad came up with a list of planning ideas, some related to LIFO sub-accounting methods, and others in the nature of long-lived temporary differences, ultimately helping the manufacturing corporation implement them.

It got messy when the Big Four firm later submitted a $1.5 million bill for the savings they produced. The manufacturer turned around and resubmitted the $1.5 million invoice to my friend's CPA firm, after all, they hadn't been doing their job as their professional advisor. I'm not positive how it finally turned out for that CPA shop, nevertheless my friend, and probably several other professionals at his firm, surely spent significant time dealing with the problem.

You might be thinking that will *never* happen to you, but if you peek at leading causes of CPA firm malpractice, failing to advise clients about opportunities makes the list.

Expansion client situations fall into a couple buckets, what I'll call the Mr. Obvious type,[xxi] and the rest.

Mr. Obvious opportunities mostly involve circumstances where your firm provides services in one functional area, such as auditing or consulting, but no others. A situation I saw numerous years ago involved a $20 million CPA firm in a major U.S. city. The managing partner was concerned about their stagnant growth, especially in the tax practice, even though their city was thriving and competing CPAs in their locale seemed to be expanding. After talking to the partners and looking at select client runs, we noted more than twenty good-sized commercial businesses, where their firm did zero tax work (only one being an SEC registrant that separated tax/audit work). More than twenty big business clients with zero tax fees! *That's* a Mr. Obvious practice expansion situation if there ever was one!

Another Mr. Obvious situation involved a very accomplished New York-based employee benefit plan audit partner that built a robust niche practice doing plan audits for a host of publicly traded companies and large private businesses, most of which were not traditional services clients at her firm. It too, would appear to be a layup to use her client list as a launch pad for introducing other services.

Expansion client situations likewise involve those time and money savings opportunities and risk-mitigating ideas your firm provides, that haven't been availed yet by your clients. Identifying these by office industry teams or functional specialists can be one of the best ways to root-out prospects. As noted, most partners in your firm will likely have a half-dozen or so expansion client possibilities.

For example, to the extent your firm goes to market by industry team, the team's leader and each client service partner could collaborate on who the best expansion client candidates are.

Besides any known opportunities by the industry leader and partner, each partner's client service team could use a service matrix to brainstorm opportunities (see below and page 121).

Manufacturing Industry Service Matrix

Service	Client A	Client B	Client C	Client D	Client E	Client F
Technology Practice						
Employer policies						
Risk review						
System appropriateness						
Data analytics:						
-Customer profit.						
-Profit density						
-Other						
Succession Services						
Estate planning						
Shareholder transition						
Retirement planning						
Investment planning						
Executive transition						
ESOP considerations						
International Tax						
Transfer pricing						
Structuring review						
Repatriation of funds						
Export incentives						
Expatriate services						
State & Local Tax						
Incentives						
Employment credits						
Sales/use nexus						

Service	Client A	Client B	Client C	Client D	Client E	Client F
Income tax nexus						
Apportionment plan.						
Protective refunds						
Unitary/combined return planning						
Property tax						
Federal Tax						
Employment credits						
Research credits						
Cost segregation						
Energy incentives						
Inventory planning						
Accounting methods:						
-Cash adoption						
-IBNR						
-Unearned rev.						
-Repair rules						
-other						
Captive insurance						
M&E reviews						
Employee Benefits						
Deferred comp.						
NQ/qualified options						
Section 409A matters						
Qualified plan review						
Fringe/other benefits						
General Risk						
Overall risk review						
Internal audit assess.						
Employee hotline						

Once ideas are identified, it's a matter of execution by the partner and service team to meet and discuss items with appropriate client personnel. Obviously, someone needs to manage the process to assure follow-up occurs. This can be either the office managing partner, industry team leader, or both.

In summary, expansion clients represent the *easiest opportunity to grow your top line*, while simultaneously strengthening relationships. As noted, most professionals with a client service mindset can participate in this growth initiative. Planning, discipline and execution are the key skills to be successful.

We'll now turn our attention to one of the often overlooked ways to stoke growth within your firm, a means that is easily within your firm's grasp with proper strategy and execution.

Emerging Issues

Every year or two, we as CPAs get gifts from Congress, accounting governing bodies, the IRS, the Treasury Department, state revenue authorities, the SEC, and a host of other regulators, depending on what industries we work in. Those gifts take the form of law or rule changes effecting our clients. Many CPA firms and their professionals often fumble the ball, and fail to realize the full value of these developments, simply because they *do not* approach implementation in a professionalized manner. Such a half-hearted approach often results in inconsistent adoption by clients, which depending on the nature of the development, can generate malpractice exposure at your shop too.

Recalling the previous discussion of what clients want in a CPA per CCH's survey, clients place great importance on their accountants being able to inform them about changing rules and regulations affecting their organizations. Most firms do an excellent job sending out client alerts, and in conducting webinars on new developments. The shortcomings often arise because the firm doesn't fully educate their own professionals on the new rules, create talking points to foster client discussions, or provide tools to aid their CPAs/clients in adopting the provisions. Further, many firms fail to distinguish that the CPA's assistance is distinct from their normal compliance services, or provide strong guidance to partners about how implementation should be priced. It's a, "you're on your own" mindset. Since the firm hasn't been strategic, what could be a multi-million dollar pop in revenue gets squandered.

Here's an approach conceived related to recent Treasury Department regulations involving the so-called repair rules. Without getting into too much detail, the Treasury Department issued temporary regulations that were going to be effective for calendar year companies in 2012 (they were later postponed and finalized in 2013). These rules had broad reach, impacting a wide swath of clients in manufacturing, construction, financial services, and real estate, as well as other commercial endeavors. Like many federal regulations, they were complex in parts, and lacking practicality in other areas. This particular emerging issues approach was designed to:

- Educate professionals exceptionally well.

- Inform clients about compliance issues, and possible accounting-related system changes that could be required.

- Create checklists, implementation programs, client discussion points, decision trees, engagement letters, marketing pieces, tax return election statements, and Form 3115 templates (for accounting method change requests) so professionals could efficiently help clients.

- Coordinate with accounting and auditing leadership to assure implementation wouldn't create GAAP complications, and industry team leaders to nuance the action plan for each specialization.

123

- Determine what specific clients were most likely to be effected, and set guidelines for expected implementation fees.

To create an emerging issues strategy, brainstorming all the possible individual items that need to occur should take place first. Next, the various tactics are "chunked" into similar components. Finally, tentative timelines are established, along with responsible parties for execution steps.

Whenever you set a strategy, there needs to be appropriate follow-up and accountability (weekly calls might be suffice for such purposes). Further, once you commence strategy execution, you'll run into unexpected items, simply because your strategy doesn't always match-up with what is happening in real life. Consequently, modifications are likely. You just need to have some degree of flexibility, but stay true to the overall goal to succeed.

You're probably thinking that crafting a multi-faceted strategy involves a lot of work, that's because *it is a lot of work*! For many emerging issues though, the work plan can be somewhat basic. Nevertheless, taking a strategic approach in the rollout of emerging issues can optimize your firm's professional services fees—while simultaneously assuring the requisite quality to lessen malpractice risks.

What if you're at a smaller firm and you lack the team bandwidth to develop tools for emerging issues? There are options. Most firms are part of an international accounting firm affiliation. It may be possible for you to organize a handful of like-minded affiliate firms to collaborate and create a combined solution to be used by each cooperating CPA shop, splitting the development effort. The firms conceivably could license or sell the solution to other affiliate members within the organization, turning it into a profit center of sorts. The point is, with creativity, there are ways for virtually all firms to build their top-line via the emerging issues plank of the E^4 Growth Method.

Who at your firm needs be involved in an emerging issues initiative? Certainly, senior professionals in the functional area or industry team need to be in the middle of creating the solution and establishing the strategy/tactics. Leadership at the firm has to lend support. Pretty much all rank and file partners and managers can be deeply involved in making it rain by delivering the emerging issue solution with your firm's existing clients.

As noted, emerging issue opportunities can involve any number of developments. In addition to tax or specilized industry law changes, items like the forthcoming revenue recognition rules per ASU 2014-09 could be "productized" to generate substantial fees as these provisions become effective. The key is to think strategically.

We'll wrap-up Chapter 5 now by focusing on the final area of the E^4 Growth Method—expanding your CPA firm via . . .

External Client Opportunities

When most CPAs think about growing their firm, they normally are contemplating organic growth via new external client opportunities. No question, it's important, and that's why we'll devote the next five chapters to various aspects of building your firm's top-line through external opportunities. Nevertheless, your firm is truly shortchanging itself to the extent you're not firing on all the previously-mentioned cylinders of the E^4 Growth Method.

If you ever needed to get yourself back into decent physical condition, you know it's a multi-faceted process. You don't just go to the health club for an hour, and say, "Okay, that'll do it, I'm good for another six months." You probably needed to hit the gym at least a few times a week, maybe mixing weight training along with cardiovascular exercises. Perhaps you hired a fitness coach for accountability. Think of building your firm's external client opportunity sales-related skills in the same vein. Just having a day or two of sales training, without further means of reinforcement to master the principles, and without modifying other aspects of your sales processes, is just wasting time and money.

How do you transform it then? You need to make an honest assessment of where you are now, what's working and what's not, how do you market your firm, what are the characteristics of your better clients, where do your new proposal opportunities come from and how successful are you in closing them, is there any meaningful tracking system of prospective client action steps, and how does your leadership team monitor it, along with discerning an approximate lifetime value of your important existing clients.

What many firms discover is that they improve external sales dramatically where they begin to:

- Proactively address limiting beliefs and common fears that inflict many professionals in sales settings.

- Emphasize personal skill-building in key areas like rapport, listening, questions, language patterns and goal setting.

- Coordinate their marketing department and professional services team's sales-related activities.

- Understand how to break through marketplace clutter that inundate most prospects.

- Articulate what really makes their firm different, what differences do those differences make, and why those differences matter to a prospect.

- Adopt a more educational, or instruction-centered marketing approach, versus one that concentrates only on their firm.

- Embrace marketing and sales efforts selectively targeting prospects that resemble your firm's best current clients—those prospects with the need for, and capability to buy greater amounts of services.

- Provide ongoing sales and influence training that reinforces and builds skills over a set timeframe.

- Build a library of case studies to serve as social proof.

- Create a sales tracking system that is managed like other key firm metrics such as chargeable time and realization.

- Have a set internal sales process when proposals do arise.

- Use restraint and discipline choosing when to bid on RFPs, particularly blind RFPs, where the buyer is principally focused on price, which can waste your firm's resources and time.

And, of course, your firm's leadership needs to have the resolve to succeed in this area.

Unraveling your firm's growth problems can solve a lot of problems and prevent a lot of headaches. Hopefully, you're seeing how availing the E^4 Growth Method can be a real difference maker. Let's move to Chapter 6 and start reflecting on those prospects you and your team need to focus on: the best potential buyers.

Chapter 5 References

[i]Trout, Jack. *Peter Drucker on Marketing.* Forbes, www.forbes.com, July 3, 2006.

[ii]Cody, Tamika. *Crowe Horwath Appoints its First Chief Innovation Officer.* Accounting Today for the WebCPA, www.accountingtoday.com, November 7, 2013.

[iii]Tysiac, Ken. *Regulation, Inflation Drove Audit Fees Higher in 2013.* Journal of Accountancy, www.journalofaccountancy.com, October 2, 2014. Note: the survey included 87 public companies, 104 private entities and 203 nonprofits according to the article.

[iv]Reichheld, Frederick F. and Teal, Thomas. *The Loyalty Effect—The Hidden Force Behind Growth, Profits and Lasting Value*. Harvard Business School Press, Boston, MA, 1996. Page 23

[v]Ibid. Pages 33 and 37-39

[vi]Ibid. Graph represents the factors on loyalty/retention on profitability—similar to the manner it appeared in the book's original printing. Page 39

[vii]Ibid. Page 42-43

[viii]Ibid. Page 43

[ix]Ibid. Pages 43-45

[x]Ibid. Pages 45-48

[xi]Ibid. Pages 48-49

[xii]Ibid. Pages 49-50

[xiii]Kidd, Bruce and Malayter, Patrick. *Avoid Losing Millions by Creating Optics on Customer "Stickiness."* PE TV with Walker Information—Part 5, BKD PE TV October 2013, www.bkd.com (7:33).

[xiv]Ibid.

[xv]Ibid.

[xvi]Ibid.

[xvii]Kidd, Bruce and Malayter, Patrick. *Avoid Losing Millions by Creating Optics on Customer "Stickiness."* PE TV with Walker Information—Part 7, BKD PE TV October 2013, www.bkd.com (3:56).

[xviii]CCH. Improving Retention through Better Client Connections. www.CCHGroup.com/ClientRetention, November, 2010. Pages 2-3, 6-7, 11-14

[xix]Ibid. Pages 12-13

[xx]Caragher, Jean Marie. *Client Retention Strategies Every CPA Firm Can Use— Are Your Clients Safe?* CPA Insider, www.cpa2biz.com, May, 11, 2011. This article reports research conducted by Bay Street Group, LLC involving client dismissals versus the CPA's view of the client's change in advisor.

[xxi]Mr. Obvious (Mr. "O") is a fictional character of the *Bob & Tom* syndicated radio show.

WHO DO YOU FOCUS ON? YOUR MARKET'S BEST POTENTIAL BUYERS, OF COURSE!

Chapter 6 highlights means of proactively growing your firm's topline using the final plank of the E^4 Growth Method, external client opportunities. When you're contemplating an external opportunities campaign, there are multiple approaches you and your firm can turn to. Irrespective of what you've done up till now, I'm advocating your marketing team and professionals devote meaningful time in the future toward attracting best buyer prospect opportunities to your firm.

Overview of the Best Buyer Philosophy

I first came across this powerful best buyer concept in a 2007 book written by the late Chet Holmes titled, *The Ultimate Sales Machine—Turbocharge Your Business with Relentless Focus on 12 Key Strategies*. Since then, I've probably purchased close to 400 copies of this book for colleagues because several of the principles can be readily adapted for accounting firms, unlike the content you'll find in most other sales-related tomes. It's a book you should *absolutely* get for your library.

Holmes points out that, "There are always a smaller number of 'best buyers' within a marketplace than the population of all buyers," consequently, it's much less expensive to market or sell to these best buyers as a subset group, versus through blasts to an enormous populous (of all possible buyers) as a means of gaining new clients.[i] Who are best buyers? These are prospective clients who have the potential need for vast levels of services, and the capacity to pay for them. They are more complex businesses and/ or sophisticated individuals than the average prospect. Equate them to the top 10 to 25 percent of your firm's essential clients, as discussed in Chapter 5. Even though these prospects may be highly coveted by your shop, *it doesn't necessarily mean they've been treated like gold by their existing provider*—often they're not.

Holmes describes such a sales and marketing focus on best buyers as a "Dream 100 effort, the 100 most promising 'best buyers' in your territory."[ii] You obviously can call the program whatever you'd like. It doesn't need to be 100 prospects either. If you're a local firm in a small town maybe it is fifteen to twenty key prospects, or if you're part of a large office with twenty partners and a diverse industry mix in a major U.S. metro area, perhaps you'll have 200 prospective clients for your team of partners and managers. We'll get into selection criteria below, for now though, think of this as a more limited number of high-value target prospects, and for sake of this discussion, we'll refer to them hereafter as either the Best Buyer 100 or just Best Buyers.

Your firm's Best Buyer 100 initiative involves an intensive marketing and sales effort to migrate each of these ideal prospects along an evolving continuum as follows:

- "I've never heard of this CPA firm," to

- "What's this CPA firm I keep hearing about," to

- "Yes, I've heard of this CPA firm," to

- "Yes, I do business with that group of professionals."[iii]

Where you and your firm can master this Best Buyer 100 approach, you'll find a meaningful jolt in revenue from very desirable clients that need and appreciate your work.

Tax Co-sourcing Best Buyer Approach

An example illustrating the compelling power behind a well-crafted Best Buyer 100 approach involved a tax co-sourcing start-up practice effort a few teammates and I originated several years ago, concentrating in Indianapolis and portions of the Chicago metro area. The focus of the initiative involved smaller capitalization U.S. publicly-traded companies and in-bound foreign entities that were traded on non-U.S. stock exchanges. I previously had experience with publicly-traded banks, my other teammates, did not. We had no Chicago office. Our Indianapolis office had publicly-traded financial services clients, but no other public companies at the time. Our practice office, however, included a rather sophisticated group of corporate tax specialists, along with large SALT and international tax units, and a dedicated research-credit team. We felt we had the mental circuitry to handle these larger clients, since on paper, the public corporations looked a lot like the private entities we served, except for who owned them.

Most of these public and foreign-based companies we targeted were served by Big Four firms. We presumed that, at least on the tax side, they were being handled by their CPA firm's B-Teams, and that the companies had limited access to their advisor's international tax and SALT professionals. We also assumed that these businesses weren't receiving top-notch service in terms of when tax returns and other projects were completed before deadlines. These expectations ultimately proved to be true.

We started a Best Buyer 100 mailing campaign to these prospects that had elements of an instruction-centered marketing technique (discussed in Chapter 7). Mailings were followed by several rounds of calls to each prospect to set up in-person appointments. During ensuing meetings, the majority of time was allotted for each prospective client to speak. They typically started out by discussing their company, what activities they principally were involved in personally, and then, what characteristics were important to them when they worked with professionals like us. What became clear from sessions, solely from the process of teeing-up quality questions and listening, were a variety of service-related gaps, and unaddressed areas where assistance was needed.

In a little more than a year, we landed ten new U.S. public companies and in-bound foreign publicly-traded entities as tax clients. Of that group, eight involved recurring financial statement tax provision and tax compliance preparation assistance, the other two were ongoing consulting and non-corporate tax compliance projects. What was *amazing* were the number of additional services opportunities ballooning from these more complex clientele, which included:

- Several ownership-change studies under IRC Section 382,

- A stock option exercise analysis, to discern how tax loss carryforwards were to be recognized for GAAP purposes

- Multiple research tax credit studies

- Various automatic and non-automatic accounting method changes for overlooked planning ideas

- Pre-distribution tax basis studies

- SALT nexus studies

- Transfer pricing assistance

- Foreign tax credit planning

- A take private transaction

- Select mergers and acquisitions

- Multiple federal and state revenue authority examination assistance projects

Many of these new clients later engaged our firm for employee benefit plan audits, another eventually became a substantial SEC audit client for our office. One of these tax co-sourcing clients became a top fee-generating firm client, due to the multiple consulting projects they requested . . . they were thrilled with the work, and happy to pay those bills because of the value received. In fact, these new clients were so active that a leadership partner at the time ultimately told us to stop bringing in new tax co-sourcing clients, because of the strain it started to put on the system. Those are good problems to have.

I hope that by now you're convinced that adopting a Best Buyer 100 initiative might make sense for developing external client opportunities.

Who Are Your Best Clients?

When you're envisioning a Best Buyer 100 program, you and your firm need to reach for prospective clientele that have the potential need for vast levels of your firm's services, with the capacity to pay for them. Preferably, some of the more complex businesses and/or sophisticated individuals in your marketplace. A great starting point in developing your target profile for a Best Buyer 100 initiative is the upper echelon of your office's or industry team's essential clients. Every firm's situation differs, of course, but examining the characteristics of the top 10 to 25 percent of your essential clients within each market likely makes sense.

Why? Presumably the best of your best have that requisite mix of complexity and sophistication, along with payment capacity. These are clients that your firm *knows how to take care of*. In short, when you contemplate working on prospective clients that are just like your VIP essential clients, there should be absolutely no doubt you can deliver.

Once you've determined your top clients, describe their characteristics. Are they:

- Multi-state

- Multi-location

- Doing business in foreign countries

- Family owned

- Facing transition issues

Other criteria such as size, industry and sub-niche also are noteworthy. Doing this will help you clarify who you're targeting.

You also could reach for Best Buyer 100 prospects that are somewhat up-market from your existing upper-echelon essential clients. Although this seems to make sense, just as it was for us with the public company tax co-sourcing initiative, it *may not* be appropriate if it involves prospects that are clearly out of your league. If you're a middle-market firm, for example, placing that local Fortune 500 Company on your list (except for perhaps loaned staffing, executive tax preparation services, or some specialty service you're providing), probably doesn't make sense.

Once you've grasped who your best clients are—and their distinguishing features, another important step involves discerning . . .

What's Their Approximate Lifetime Value?

The lifetime value of a current upper echelon essential client is a useful thought exercise for you and your team to entertain. It's the non-present valued stream of profits one of these prime clients delivers through their relationship with your firm.[IV] If, on average, one of these clients pays $100,000 a year at your normal realization rate, and your firm's operating income ratio to gross income is 40 percent, then the approximate annual value of the client is $40,000. If your average top client maintains a twelve-year relationship with your shop, the lifetime value is $480,000. Go through this mental process with several upper-tier clients—it's fine to do an approximation since you're not looking for absolute accuracy.

So, what's the benefit of doing this? Accumulating this data on lifetime value:

- Emphasizes just how important acquiring new clientele in this category is, as opposed to just pursuing anyone in the market.

- Puts proper perspective on how irrelevant start-up cost are in the greater scheme of a long-term relationship.

- Reinforces the need to take great care of your firm's existing flock of essential clients.

Now, while you're still contemplating these more significant essential clients, your teammates and you need to think through . . .

How Have You Helped Them?

As you're reflecting on these best of your best clients, it's important for you and your team to identify some of the ways you've helped them in significant ways. What are some of the methods your firm has employed to save them time or money, such as tax planning ideas or other strategic business advice, and how have you assisted them in alleviating risks? With these top clients, you should have a **big** list.

Craft "FIRM" Case Studies

Once you're armed with this background knowledge for specific key clients, it's time to create case studies. To the extent that you're targeting Best Buyer 100 prospects that look like the upper echelon of your essential clients, it's only logical that these prospects will want to know about how your firm and you have delivered. Specifically, how you've delivered these services to other businesses or individuals who are *just* like them. You'll be able to accomplish that by harnessing the power of social proof as discussed in Chapter 3 by generating multiple FIRM case studies.

A FIRM case study is a story about a particular circumstance, where your shop has saved a client significant money or time in operations, or assisted them in alleviating meaningful risk. In this story, you highlight the:

- **Facts:** Provide background about the client in a generic fashion.

- **Issues:** What were the client's *specific* business problems or challenges?

- **Resolution:** What creativity or value-add did your professionals and you bring to the table to generate a favorable client outcome.

- **Why it Mattered:** Outline the great consequences that arose from the problems/issues your firm handled.

Most CPAs are fairly humble souls, and don't like to brag about the good stuff they've done at work (unless, of course they're around other CPAs). In drafting your FIRM case studies, you need to bury the humility. Many CPAs that have been in the profession for several years might not view elements of their great service as necessarily being "special." I'm *not* suggesting that you crow about how you've cut someone's tax bill by having claimed accelerated depreciation, or something basic like that. If you've prevailed in a complex state or federal revenue exam (e.g., after the government initially proposed unbearable tax adjustments), *that* may be worth capturing as a FIRM case study—as are most planning projects that will generate significant future savings.

Here are a handful of hypothetical situations that could be developed into FIRM case studies for a fictional accounting firm we'll call the ABC CPA Firm ("ABC"):

- **Deviation Cost Segregation Studies Wallop an Unexpected Tax Bill:** This New Jersey-headquartered multi-state men's retail clothing store was facing stout federal/state extension payments after robust holiday sales and an extraordinary gain. ABC's corporate tax professionals, along with the engineering-based cost segregation group conducted deviation cost segregation depreciation studies on the nearly 50 mall-based stores placed in service since the year 2000. Combining the cost segregation project with special automatic accounting method change rules produced a nearly $6 million current federal/state tax reduction—and a huge smile from this ownership team's CFO!

- **Saving a $900,000 Benefit:** This Minneapolis-based, privately-owned manufacturing company's Big Four tax advisor inadvertently failed to make a timely DISC election— notwithstanding such accounting firm quarterbacking all other aspects to implement the export incentive. ABC discovered such oversight in connection with a complimentary "tax return physical," noting that the advisor's error would cost the company nearly $900,000. ABC, working with the company and its legal counsel, crafted a private letter ruling requesting the ability to retroactively make such IC-DISC election. After multiple conferences with IRS National Office, the request was granted, and the intended $900,000 in tax savings preserved!

- **Transfer Pricing Becomes a Global Tax Planning Tool:** Many businesses view transfer pricing as a compliance burden versus a planning tool. This Seattle-based multinational manufacturer had over $1.8 million of foreign tax credit carryovers—struggling to find means to utilize this valuable asset. ABC's international group reviewed intercompany transactions between the U.S. parent and its foreign subsidiaries—assessing the economic elements to the relationship. Based on such analysis, intercompany agreements were revised to take into account the additional identified risks/functions of the parent corporation—along with adjustments for new intangible assets utilized by the foreign subsidiaries. Updated transfer prices were established for intangibles, tangibles and services, in accordance with U.S. and foreign country transfer pricing guidelines. As a result of ABC's work product, the corporate group will realize a $2.4 million reduction in income taxes over the next four years, including full utilization of the unused foreign credits within the statutory carryforward period.

- **Property Tax Abatement Reducing "Real" Capital Costs:** This west coast manufacturer of consumer home products was contemplating setting up new production lines due to growing product demand. In studying their situation, ABC learned that although product demand was expanding, raw material costs were likewise increasing exponentially. Armed with this raw material cost knowledge, as well as data on foreign competition in the marketplace, ABC's SALT professionals were able to broker nearly $400,000 in immediate property tax relief with local officials to soothe the sting from the capital outlay.

Conceivably, summaries like those above can then be broadened or expanded upon using the FIRM approach to ultimately resemble the case study highlighted in Chapter 3. This is precisely the type of approach that was done in creating marketing documents for the previously-noted tax co-sourcing initiative.

If you are preparing case studies involving federal tax examples, you are *required* to obtain authorization from the client-taxpayer pursuant to IRC Section 7216, with harsh penalties for failure to comply. See Appendix A for a sample authorization request form that is suitable for federal tax purposes. For non-tax case studies, it obviously makes sense to obtain client consent too to utilize their specific situation in any sales and marketing effort.

Let's dispel another notion held by many CPAs. A number of accountants *won't want to even ask* clients to approve a case study for marketing purposes, because they perceive the client will say "no" (i.e., they are fearful the client will reject them). I can think of 35 to 40 requests teammates made to obtain client sign-offs for case studies, and 100 percent of those clients said "yes." Of course you need to generalize certain aspects of their facts to appropriately disguise the client. You need to be sensible in describing how you resolved their situation. You need to be flexible and make requested edits to appease the client. Nevertheless, when you've done great things to help a client, they are normally delighted to reciprocate and assist you, too.

No doubt, capturing this type of data requires top-of-mind awareness from individuals at your firm, because it takes time, effort and discipline to continuously gather stories. A technique that some firms use to accomplish this task involves adding a client success stories agenda item to monthly partner-manager meetings. In the end, it will be worth it when you roll out your Best Buyer 100 program, as you'll have plenty of social proof examples to impress prospects with. Even though you may be somewhat skeptical right now, at most firms there are likely many heroic stories that happen with your upper-end essential clientele each year. Start capturing these accounts from your professionals, and begin using them to your firm's advantage.

Approaches to Identifying Your Market's Best Buyer 100

Once you're clear on your Best Buyer 100 criteria, it's time to match results against the potential prospects in your marketplace. How you define your marketplace is unique to each firm and practice team, depending on where you regularly serve or pursue clients. If you run a specialty practice like the transactions team I've described previously, the marketplace for new clients could broadly be deemed as the entire U.S. For a more general group such as a tax co-sourcing practice, where location matters to prospects, the market territory likely would be much narrower.

The industries you're pursuing impact the ease of gathering prospect data too. In most regulated industries like banking, insurance, healthcare and nonprofit colleges/universities, for example, there are enormous amounts of data available for you to track and study to determine Best Buyer 100 targets. In fact, it's often easy to see actual financial statement data on these entities via trade-related surveys and other independent consulting firm publications. Background info normally is available in such sources about each organization's leadership team too. Where you're working in a regulated industry, you probably already know where in your state to find the best reference sources.

The world becomes a *lot* murkier where your Best Buyer 100 initiative is directed at non-public companies in industries like manufacturing, distribution, construction, real estate, technology, and general business services. For these types of businesses, a good starting point might be *Dun & Bradstreet*'s publication company "Hoovers," although some marketing folks report there can be challenges with the accuracy and completeness of its data. You may be able to refine such a preliminary Hoovers list through comparisons with your state's applicable industry association database. Likewise, local bankers, business-focused attorneys, and commercial insurance professionals in your community might be capable network sources for improving your Best Buyer 100 list's accuracy, or may be helpful in augmenting it. Asking your top echelon essential clients which companies or business people they most respect in town also could provide valuable input in preparing your ultimate targets. Building a great prospect database, with non-public and non-regulated companies is a process, it's not as easy as flipping a switch. Getting started is key, followed by attention to preparing regular list updates.

Just as discerning *what* prospects make your Best Buyer 100 list is imperative, deciding who the best contact is at each company is also critically important for you and your firm. According to Chet Holmes, "You need to choose the point of contact at the company having the authority to say 'Yes.' Oftentimes a targeted individual has the ability to deal out a 'No,' but needs to go higher up the organizational structure to gain 'an approval.' Where that's the case, you need to be approaching that higher-level individual."[v] In many transaction services marketing initiatives, the vice president level would be targeted, as opposed to directors and partners at a private equity firms, because the VPs actually decide who vets their deals. At public companies, tax co-sourcing assignments were normally awarded by a firm's CFO, so they would be the prospect target. At many privately-owned companies, the CEO or owner is the person who pays the bills, and probably is the ultimate decision maker.

When you and your firm are concentrating on a CEO-level person and other executives at a target prospect, the message needs to be *truly captivating*. That's where "instruction-centered marketing," Chapter 7's focus, can help you shine.

Chapter 6 References

[i]Holmes, Chet. *The Ultimate Sales Machine—Turbocharge Your Business with Relentless Focus on 12 Key Strategies*. Penguin Group (USA) Inc., New York, NY, 2007. Page 102

[ii]Ibid. Page 103

[iii]Ibid. Page 103

[iv]The concept of "lifetime value of a client" was first introduced to me from marketing/sales advisor Jay Abraham—although multiple others have written on this topic. See: Abraham, Jay. *Getting Everything You Can Out of All You've Got*. Truman Talley Books, St. Martin's Press, New York, NY, 2000. Pages 70-72.

[v]Op. cit. Holmes. Page 176

CHAPTER 7

INSTRUCTION-CENTERED MARKETING AS A DIFFERENTIATOR

Here are two questions to consider for a moment. What do you want your fellow professionals to accomplish when they meet with prospects, and when they interact in the market?

You: That's a silly question, Patrick. We want to drive new business.

Me: Is that all you want to accomplish?

You: What else is there?

Me: If you approach sales and marketing strategically instead of just tactically, there are many other goals you could consider. For example:

- "Would you like your firm to be respected?

- Do you want the marketplace or your prospects to trust you?

- Would it make sense to preempt claims or pricing promises that could be made by an incumbent or competing firm?

- Would you like your professionals to be perceived as experts?

- Would you want your team to be viewed as influential?

- Do you want the prospect to be decisive, and feel a sense of urgency to consider your firm?

You: Certainly. *All* those make sense"[i]

Me: They absolutely are worthwhile aims, but you'll *never* accomplish any of them unless you approach marketing and sales from a broad, strategic perspective versus tactical standpoint.

So before honing-in on accomplishing strategic goals via instruction-centered marketing, let's visit:

The Buying Pyramid—Those Buying Now Versus All Others

We've discussed this a bit in Chapter 5, when highlighting risks associated with essential clients. Chet Holmes' research surrounding buyer characteristics within a host of products and services concluded the following general behavioral classifications apply to a set population of prospective clients:[ii]

Chet Holmes Model

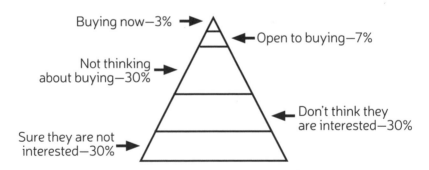

Buying now—3%
Open to buying—7%
Not thinking about buying—30%
Don't think they are interested—30%
Sure they are not interested—30%

According to Holmes' analysis, "3 percent of prospective clients are 'buying now', which is where predominately all commerce is occurring."[iii] In the CPA world, many cases falling into this category are traditional RFPs that could involve a few proposing firms, including the incumbent CPA shop. Normally, these are *highly* competitive situations, and have a way of being commoditized by the prospective client, with price unfortunately, being one of the main differentiators.

In Holmes' breakdown, "7 percent of this potential class of prospects are open to the notion of buying. This is the percentage who may be dissatisfied with their current provider, and are not opposed to change, but who may not yet be buying now."[iv]

The 90-percent remainder represents, three equal categories, with the top third being a group that for whatever reason, just isn't thinking about it. They're not opposed to making a change in advisor, but not committed to getting a new accounting provider either, they are simply not thinking about it. Where such a prospective client receives most traditional CPA firm marketing material, it likely would have zero impact because, they are just not thinking about a CPA firm change.

Holmes' perception of the next third is that they "Think they are not interested;" they are not neutral like the aforementioned 30-percent group. The final group is a class of prospects that Holmes views as being definitely not interested. This last group is either completely happy with their existing relationship, or conceivably, don't know what they don't know with respect to their company's accounting or advisory services or service provider.[v]

Let's compare the foregoing with the Walker Research and CCH survey data from Chapter 5.[vi]

Walker Research Customer Risk Model

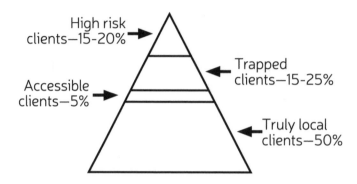

As previously described, high-risk clients represent clientele that are unhappy and will be gone soon, assuming there isn't action taken to repair aspects of the relationship.

Trapped clients are existing patrons that need their advisor's services, they are using the provider because they have to have the service performed, but they might or might not be utilizing them a year from now. These clients are often not utilizing the breadth of services the CPA's firm offers.

According to Walker's analysis, truly loyal clients view the advisor as their partner, they value their CPA's services, repelling competitors that call on them, and spend meaningful larger amounts with their firm than do other clientele. Accessible clients have similar characteristics to the truly loyal classification, but possibly could change accounting firms due to factors beyond your firm, and the client's, control.

Let's shift gears to the CCH client survey results:

CCH Analysis of CPA Client Risk

Clients that are highly likely to change—15%

Clients that are somewhat likely to change—21%

Satisfied clients— no stated notion to change CPA firms—47%

Completely satisfied clients—17%

As highlighted in Chapter 5, CCH's work notes that gaps exist between client expectations for their CPA firm's performance on key criteria, versus their firm's actual performance. Consequently, only 17 percent of business clients noted they were *completely satisfied with their accountant or advisor.* Surveyed business clients further indicated that 15 percent were "very likely" to change accounting firms, whereas another 21 percent stated they were "somewhat likely" to change firms. CCH concluded that most clients won't tell their CPA they are dissatisfied unless specifically asked, they'll just stop doing business with them.

Amalgamating the preceding data with my experience and personal judgment, here's my take on prospect approachability:

Malayter's Perception of CPA Client Risk/Prospect Receptivity in Marketplace

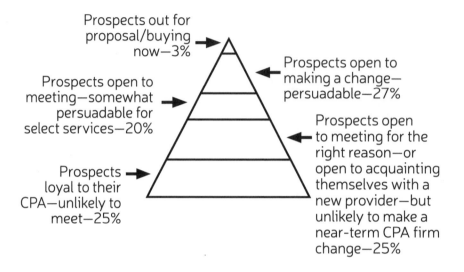

Prospects out for proposal/buying now—3%

Prospects open to making a change—persuadable—27%

Prospects open to meeting—somewhat persuadable for select services—20%

Prospects open to meeting for the right reason—or open to acquainting themselves with a new provider—but unlikely to make a near-term CPA firm change—25%

Prospects loyal to their CPA—unlikely to meet—25%

Some might quibble with a few percentages one way or the other, and obviously, on any given day, prospects may shift their perceptions about their advisor. Yet there are more consistencies than differences among the charts. As someone who's been on the frontline of making things happen in the marketplace for years, *there are far wider openings than you might think* to create revenue-producing relationships with prospective clients. Significant openings, provided your firm and you are elegant and educational in your marketplace message and persistent in attacking the market.

One final data point of note comes from Mike Schultz, John Doerr, and Lee Frederiksen's 2013 book, *Professional Services Marketing—How the Best Firms Build Premier Brands, Thriving Lead Generation Engines, and Cultures of Business Development Success.* The authors note that in the professional services context, "Buyers are *ready* to switch. The openness to switching to a new provider represents a huge opportunity for the leaders of professional services businesses. It's an opportunity for those who are willing to do what it takes to convince buyers to work with a new firm: theirs!"[vii]

The authors likewise note that leads typically sort into three buckets, "with 25 percent being short-term leads, 25 percent constituting bad-fits, and the remainder falling into a longer-term slot. Longer-term can range from 3- to 24-month cycles, however, the authors sense this extended timeframe represents a necessary gap for both the CPA firm and the prospect company to be in the right position and time to buy. Once the prospect becomes 'ready,' the actual sales cycle can be months or less."[viii]

So, with that background on what your marketplace looks like—and the composition of prospects, let's shift our attention to . . .

The Case for Instruction-centered Marketing

Depending on which of the models you embrace from the prior section, there are only a limited number of prospects—only about 3 percent or so, are actually buying now, or in the market for a new provider at any given time. With the overload of information vying for a prospect's attention, does it make sense to you that many traditional marketing pieces flying out of accounting firms sail right past the eyes of most prospects?

What can you do to be more strategic, grab the attention of a larger chunk of those businesses, and keep it long enough to make a positive impression? How can your firm drive market messages that appeal not just to those buying now, but to those potential clients that are open to changing and persuadable, and conceivably, even to those prospects who are loyal to their existing CPAs and not predisposed to swapping-out providers? The way to accomplish it involves a concept I call instruction-centered marketing.

Instruction-centered marketing goes by a lot of different names, some call it education-based marketing or content marketing, while others label it as custom publishing, private media, and branded storytelling. Joe Pulizzi, author of *Epic Content Marketing*, contrasts this approach from other methods by noting, "Traditional marketing has always been about getting services in front of the right audience, whereas instruction-centered marketing is about meeting the informational needs of prospective clients so they become interested in you. Prospects frankly don't care about you or your service offerings, *they care about themselves*. Content/ instruction-centered marketing is all about creating interesting information your potential clients are passionate about, so they actually pay attention to you. The objective is to create and distribute valuable and compelling content/data to a clearly defined and understood target audience, to drive profitable prospect or client actions. The material can be informative, engaging, or amusing. However, it has to have the focus on motivating prospect action. It's communicating, and clearly is persuasive, but doesn't come across as 'selling' per se."[ix]

Authors Schultz, Doerr, and Frederiksen's slant on this marketing approach is that it "takes thought leadership to a different plane, raising the expertise profile of the entire firm." Specifically, they note that, "When you help prospective clients understand how to overcome a complex business problem, they appreciate the intelligence of your methodology. It enables potential clients to sample your thinking and approach, expands a firm's market reach via distributed content that is searchable, is arguably less expensive than many forms of traditional marketing, and is a natural for CPAs and other professional services firms."[x]

One of the early adopters to this marketing style to expand the range of prospects was the above-noted Chet Holmes, using the method he termed "education-based marketing." Through an assortment of clients and industries, he observed that, "By providing some degree of education value to prospects, you have greater opportunity to attract more potential buyers and develop greater credibility." Likewise, he found it "opened doors to a vast portion of his population of potential buyers, the entire scope of the buyers' pyramid, versus those just buying now. To the extent you come from a place of being perceived as a market or industry expert, as opposed to just an audit or tax professional, means that you'll be deemed to be more skilled and knowledgeable than most competitors with a one-track mind who simply want to sell."[xi] An instruction-centered approach can conceivably:

- Foster greater respect

- Increase appointments

- Build trust

- Preempt competitor claims

- Create an aura of expertise

- Enhance influence

- Expedite a prospect's decision-making process in your firm's favor

We'll look at a few different examples of using an instruction-centered marketing methodology to pursue Best Buyers. Arguably, the only limitations though on possible approaches are based on the confines of you or your firm's imagination.

Example #1: Private Equity Focused White Paper

Several years ago, not long after I learned about instruction-centered marketing methods, my teammates and I crafted a private-equity focused document titled, "*Seven Treacherous Trends Impacting PE Firms—How to Avoid the Pitfalls to Prosperity*." At the time, we were striving to make a name for ourselves in a crowded market of CPA providers to such industry. The financial crises had walloped PE investing, and caused many investment groups to be internally-focused on portfolio company matters. Calling up PE firm professionals, and trying to set up meetings related to their transaction advisory-related needs, would be met with a "click" from the other end of the phone. Setting meetings to highlight the results of our team's recent study on *Seven Treacherous Trends*, however, appealed to a far-reaching segment of the PE market.

The resulting instruction-centered research document was a twenty-page white paper with graphs and references, and included the following topics:

The Real Truth, Unemployment at 21 Percent: This focused on how, at the end of 2009, the seasonally-adjusted U-3 unemployment rate—or the official unemployment rate— was calculated at 9.97 percent, whereas the broader December 2009 U-6 unemployment rate stood at 17.3 percent. Of real concern though was that, during the Clinton Administration, "discouraged workers," those who had given up looking for a job because there were no jobs to be had, were reclassified, and counted only if they had been discouraged for less than a year. This time qualification essentially cut out long-term discouraged workers from the U-6 determination. By using an apples-to-apples comparison, a fully-loaded unemployment estimate of 21.9 percent existed as of December 2009, versus what the Bureau of Labor Statistics reported. The effect on consumer spending was discussed, along with the effect on PE investments.

Consumer Spending Cycle and the Aging Baby Boomer: Described how nearly 30 percent of the U.S. population, the Baby Boomer generation, whose importance is not only because of its size, but also its wealth, was on the brink of retirement. The implications on consumer-related portfolio companies was emphasized.

Painful Implications of Tax Policy in a Soak the Rich Environment: Highlighted how multiple tax proposals teed up by the Obama administration and Congress could potentially effect economic growth. New taxes related to the Affordable Care Act, changes related to carried interest taxation (a hot-button issue to PE firms), a new proposed bank tax, proposals to significant increase income subject to Social Security tax, and a host of new state-imposed fees and levies were discussed.

Oops—Sorry We Missed It Guys! Discussed how one way PEGs use to protect their portfolio company investments and mitigate risk—the annual independent audit by a CPA firm, frequently has gaping holes in it based on PCAOB inspection reports and results from insurance company claims.

The Troubling Rise in White Collar Fraud: Overviewed compounding challenges PEGs face in owning businesses in a difficult economy and described an environment leading to a rise in the three most prevalent fraud predicators: pressure, opportunity, and the ability to rationalize illegal behavior, collectively known as the fraud triangle.

An Avalanche of PEG Dry Powder Chasing Fewer Quality Deals: Articulated the gargantuan amount of time-sensitive committed capital currently awaiting investment, along with the considerable risk of overpayment existing.

Institutional Investors Rethinking PE Allocations: Described how many university endowments, retirement funds, and other institutional investors were reevaluating and reallocating monies to more traditional securities from so-called alternative investments, including private equity, as well as the potential implications on future fund-raising.

A short PowerPoint was used in meetings with prospects to keep the discussion on task.

Think for a moment: would a conversation about topics like those described above have appeal to a broader audience of prospects, as opposed to calling-up folks to talk about your firm's services, or just to meet? You bet!

Example #2: Using a Niche Issue to Approach Multi-Industry Best Buyers

Employing instruction-centered marketing using a niche issue to familiarize Best Buyer prospects with your firm (and arguably create other traditional service openings) can be an effective strategy. An illustrative topic for this approach could involve risk management. Since risk management matters are both broad and the type of concern that unfortunately impacts all types of entities, it may well be powerful in a multi-industry Best Buyer effort. Your firm's or industry team's activities could include:

- An introductory series of contacts (e.g., letters, emails and calls) with a call-to-action to attend a firm-sponsored complimentary online seminar (e.g., with litigation defense counsel or insurance experts participating along with your shop's specialists) describing recent trends.

- Select letters offering a premium white paper describing the five most prominent monetary risks impacting enterprises in your region—and means to mitigate them.

- A contact with sanitized case studies highlighting self-imposed financial penalties companies face by ignoring the forewarnings of risks and failing to take corrective action.

- Issuing a complimentary "litigation risk-assessment questionnaire" generated by your firm—or tailoring documents from other organizations to Best Buyer prospects—with your professionals reviewing the responses and offering suggestions.

- Providing instruction-centered guidance highlighting best practices to deter common risks—including risks within the accounting/financial functions.

- Establishing meetings to discuss each Best Buyer entity's risk profile with a local office partner and/or litigation services-forensics professional, if applicable.

Would your firm get rich off this one niche issue campaign? Probably not! What it could provide, though, is an excellent opportunity to generate relationships with future Best Buyer clients, where there hadn't been one before—and give your professionals a constructive reason to maintain contact with such folks on an ongoing basis.

Note: interactions with your firm's essential clients surrounding their key business concerns/worries might be helpful in identifying other niche issues of interest to Best Buyer prospects for future instruction-centered marketing campaigns too.

Example #3: Tax Services to Drive Best Buyer Prospect Opportunities

As discussed in preceding chapters, tax is often *the* hot button issue with many companies, so that a well-crafted tax-oriented Best Buyer initiative can definitely resonate in the marketplace.

Here is a hypothetical example strategy you and your firm can consider implementing. A campaign like this would be focused principally on the M&D industry and commercial companies.

Rollout Strategy for a Tax-focused Best Buyer Instruction - centered Marketing Campaign

Date: Feb. 1st	Date: Feb. 14th	Date: Feb 25th	March 5th
Snail mail/email letter Buffett letter on "relationships" also send out RCPs* Best Buyer prospects	Email letter only Tax TV** feature on new "repair rules" Best Buyer prospects and existing clients	Snail mail only Tax TV DVD on new "repair rules" and prior RCPs Best Buyer prospects	Call to action: tax physical review Best Buyer prospects
Date: March 14th Snail mail/email letter "Jaws theme", plus RCPs with SALT focus Best Buyer prospects	**Date: March 25th** Email letter only Tax TV feature: SALT "Ignorance isn't Bliss" Best Buyers and clients	**Date: April 4th** Snail mail only Tax TV DVD on SALT matters and prior RCPs Best Buyer prospects	**Date:** **April 4th to 10th** Call to action: free SALT nexus review questionnaire Best Buyers/clients too
Date: April 16th Snail mail/email letter International focus, also send RCPs with international emphasis Best Buyer prospects	**Date: April 25th** Email letter only Tax TV session on ITS planning and transfer pricing issues Best Buyers and clients	**Date: May 6th** Snail mail (consider email too) Tax TV DVD on international and RCPs Best Buyer prospects	**Date May 6-15th** Call to action for complimentary ITS "tax physical review"
Date: May 16th Snail mail/email letter, with RCPs Accounting methods/ other planning issues Best Buyer prospects	**Date: May 28th** Email letter only Tax TV session on accounting methods, and other tax planning Best Buyers and clients	**Date: June 9th** Snail mail Tax TV DVD on tax planning and accounting methods Best Buyers prospects	**Date: All June** Call for action on "tax physicals" for Best Buyers, aggressive calling campaign for in-person meetings

* RCPs are recently completed projects representing tax savings produced from planning. Please see the discussion in Chapter 6 related to FIRM case studies.

** Tax TV is an informative video program recorded by specialists in a particular subject area, and highlights important-to-know issues and planning matters. Your firm could construct its own alternative.

Several clarification points of note:

1. Carrying out an instruction-centered marketing campaign requires advanced planning and commitment to staying on task. Things can get messy if you fail to plan and let the schedule slip.

2. I'm not suggesting that you eliminate all your other historic marketing approaches. Since this is new to most of you, approach this as a beta test, a *very serious* beta test.

3. You might be asking yourself, "Won't this be expensive to pull off?" Again, you're focusing on a limited number of prospects, the Best Buyers. Virtually any CPA firm can easily afford this.

4. This particular type of plan should be slated during a time frame when Best Buyer prospects are presumably highly focused on tax-related matters. A campaign of this nature could also be run in August or September as many prominent businesses file returns on an extended basis.

5. Some of you might think this approach is overkill, a dozen or more contacts in a four months, plus calls, but, *they'll definitely know who you are by the time you are calling for appointments*, and most will admire the tenacity.

6. The letters or emails you'll be sending will involve stories or other aspects designed to draw the reader in. Remember, Best Buyer prospects frankly don't care about you or your service offerings, *they care about themselves.* The material can be informative, engaging or amusing, but, it ultimately has to have focus on motivating prospect Best Buyer action.

Industry-grounded Approach

Finding messages or topics that resonate within an entire population of CPA firm Best Buyer prospects will likely be tough, that's why many accounting and advisory firms go to market by concentrating on specific industry niches. Perhaps with the exception of a few subject areas, like risk management, it can be truly difficult to find hot-button issues appealing to the entire swath of your firm's Best Buyer prospects. Issues in the marketplace impacting banks are likely unique from those effecting construction companies, colleges, and hospitals. Consequently, to have relevance with your instruction-centered marketing campaigns, tailoring campaigns on an industry basis would be a smart tactic. Presumably, your industry team leaders have sufficient domain knowledge to craft a compelling content- or education-based narrative about issues impacting Best Buyer prospects in their niche (or at minimum, be able to identify *what the issues are* for other teammates, or perhaps outside consultants to develop content material).

Pain-driven Messages

What newsflash is likely to garner more of your attention: that beautiful weekend weather is expected, or Hurricane Patrick is expected to hit land on Saturday? My guess is the hurricane, because for most people, pain-driven messages carry much greater importance, simply because humans are hardwired to avoid painful consequences and are more motivated to sidestep pain, versus seeking pleasure. There is potentially important action needed on your part to avoid that pain. So, when you're crafting instruction-centered marketing deliverables, you and your firm will want to keep that thought in mind.

Here are a few additional comparisons:

Flaccid Dispatch	Pain-oriented Attention Grabber
Treasury Issues New Repair Rules	New IRS Rules: Take Action or You May Pay Thousands
Three Things Iowa Pig Farmers Should Know	How Iowa Pig Farmers Can Avoid the Slop Now!
Retirement Planning Steps to Assure Comfort	Avoid Eating Dog Food During Your Retirement Years!

Your firm's marketing department will no doubt be more eloquent than the above examples by yours truly, but hopefully you're getting a sense of how pain-driven communications have a *far better chance* of getting through the clutter.

Headlines and Opening Sentences: Why These Matters

When crafting marketing letters, emails, and other deliverables, you're surely thinking about how to make a positive impression on your Best Buyers. *What you should also be thinking about is their need to reduce the distractions in their lives*, and how they may currently be doing that. Many executives and professionals sort their snail mail in close proximity to their office's trash can. Most things that smell like junk mail fly right into that can. Online it's pretty much the same drill. You have a split-second to catch their attention, favorably, or you're deleted. So here are a few tips in creating communications that survive, and make the reader's job easier:

- If you're using a headline in a letter or subject line in your email, it must be one that catches their attention. Roughly five times as many people read a headline versus the body of an article, email, or letter.[xii]

- In letters and emails, beyond the headline, the first sentence and paragraph garners the most attention. That needs to draw the reader in, too.

- An important facet of gaining attention is to use the prospect's name, as opposed to general salutation. I prefer using someone's first name, versus Mr. Jones.

- If you're concerned about someone not reading through an entire document, consider using bold font to draw out the key portions of an article, email, or letter. By doing so, their eyes will naturally be pulled to those phrases or sentences. The following is an example of a recent marketing letter:

Dear John:

With the turn of the calendar to 2015, the nation's political attention will soon be shifting to the forthcoming presidential election cycle. Surely, a number of historical topics will be debated, including taxes, education, and immigration, along with new topics like economic inequality.

One topic that won't be on the agenda, though, involves the degree of inequality among U.S. accounting firms, and how the rich are apparently getting richer, and the poor, poorer. How? If you analyze the topline growth patterns of leading CPA firms, you'll see some rather compelling patterns.

Adjusting for major mergers, such as the CliftonLarsonAllen, Dixon Hughes Goodman and CohnResnick fusions, and the Plante Moran/Blackman Kallick combination, top-quartile growers expanded at an average and median rate of 14.3 percent and 13.4 percent for the past three-year span, whereas bottom quartile growth firms approximated 0.6 percent and 1.5 percent during such timeframe, respectively. Third quartile growth firms struggled, too, with an average three-year growth rate of roughly 5.2 percent. One great aspect of you being a CPA, is that you understand financial principles like the Rule of 72, and how firms in the two lower quartiles are speeding down the highway of irrelevance, if these trends continue.

Subnormal growth creates many other headaches, besides just irrelevance, including:

- Limiting the ability to add net new partners, causing the potential loss of high-potential staff.

- Net-income-per-partner pressures that can impede your desire to invest in new services.

- Constraints on funding retirement-related payouts, that create roadblocks to remaining independent.

Based on our review of relevant *Accounting Today Top 100/ Regional Leaders'* Growth Data Reports for each of the three years ending in March 2014, **your firm's organic growth appeared to approximate ___%, or within the third quartile**. As the captain of your ship, you obviously have lots of hats to wear, but if you've resolved to attack this sluggish growth matter now, we'd love to offer our perspectives and assistance.

CPA Growth Partners provides a comprehensive methodology to stoke massive growth at your CPA firm, the E^4 Growth Method, an approach that involves all your professionals. *Please contact me at 317.413.7538 or Pmalayter@cpagrowthpartners.com to schedule a cost-free initial consultation.*

Warmly,
Patrick M. Malayter, CPA, Founder

Although the above memo didn't include the depth of most instruction-centered marketing documents, it did contain many pertinent elements, such as relevant market data, as well as facts about the XYZ CPA firm's comparative position. It likewise had pain-oriented news in terms of consequences to the reader and an imbedded call out via the use of bold font.

Modes to Drive Your Messages

Presuming you've created great content, how do you get it in the hands of the folks you want to see it? There are myriad options out there, and to the extent you're focused on a well-defined group of Best Buyers, your distribution strategy can be streamlined and fairly basic. Even with a broad marketing initiative, versus the narrow Best Buyer approach advocated herein, "Research shows that firms that allocate 40 to 60 percent of their marketing resources to traditional offline techniques tend to perform at their peak, with the balance devoted to online methods."[xiii] In the world of approaching Best Buyer Prospects, here are the most effective forms from my experience:

Snail mail: Many inside professional services firms underrate the power of traditional direct mail to target key prospects. The accountant in you probably leans on the notion that it's considerably cheaper to use email, but frankly, snail mail can be *highly* effective. In fact, with the volume of regular mail in B-to-B settings having fallen off a cliff in recent years, getting genuine U.S. postage at work is perceived as unique or novel by many recipients. Several marketing thought leaders suggest well-crafted direct mail has strong ability to break through the clutter and reach the most significant executives at prospects—some point out it can double or triple the effectiveness of your sales initiatives. Pay attention to the good hygiene tips involving headlines, first names, and selectively using bold font per the above discussion. Furthermore, consider using a real first class U.S. postage stamp. It sets your letter apart in that it doesn't look like bulk-rate third class junk mail, increasing the chance it will be opened. In scheduling your snail mail campaign, make sure your team and you clean-up the mailing list. Misspellings can end up landing back at your office, or worse offending the recipient.

Email marketing: As noted, many firms have replaced snail mail with email marketing approaches. On the positive side, besides cost, various email tools and service providers have created data-analytics capabilities to help discern the opening and click-through rates of recipients. Email enables distribution of other unique content, such as videos and extensive white papers that aren't possible with snail mail. Email deliverability, however, is getting more problematic with ever-increasing spam filter technology, so your IT professionals need to be abreast of potential content flags and the peculiarities of evolving email delivery systems. Similar to snail mail, taking time to build an accurate distribution list is critical, or you'll struggle with the garbage-in/garbage-out phenomenon.

Videos: Video is extremely effective to disseminate valuable content quickly, and can help your team make a rich impression on prospects. It allows prospects to see your firm's personality. High quality videos can be produced and edited inexpensively and can either be distributed via email or burned onto DVDs and shipped to Best Buyer prospects through snail mail, or both ways simultaneously. As discussed in Chapter 3, with our private-equity focused service arena, teammates and I filmed interviews with several Best Buyer prospects as thought leaders. Many later became clients.

Private webinars: Webinars, limited to a select group of Best Buyers, or perhaps that include your firm's Essential Clients too, are terrific to build credibility via demonstrating expertise. It can help your prospects and clients educate themselves on topics critical to their business. Since you're hopefully wanting to be perceived as a thought leader versus Joe Salesman, keep the discussion educational. Post-presentation, add the recorded version of the webinar to your website and email the link to all attendees for future reference, as well as to all those Best Buyers who couldn't attend.

Telephone tactics: These are essential to building Best Buyer relationships. It is critical to making introductions to Best Buyers, and enhancing connections once initiated. If you think you can offload this process to a call center or some junior professional at your shop, think again.

Eyeball-to-eyeball meetings with Best Buyer prospects: Some may view this as an end product of the preceding five modes of driving your message. Having a live session with your Best Buyer prospect is truly critical, and executing on the above marketing modes often is a precursor to meeting eyeball-to-eyeball. In-person meetings are one of the few opportunities to have a prospect's undivided attention. *That's why they are musts.* In a study of the fastest growing professional services firms in the U.S., "personal visits to prospects" was designated as one of the preferred marketing modes of high-growth firms, as opposed to their below-average and average-growth compatriots.[xiv] We'll discuss approaches for these sessions in Chapters 8-10.

There are many other marketing approaches available from traditional networking activities to newer online means such as blogging, search engine optimization, and social media approaches. Those are all great, too. With a narrow, well-targeted Best Buyer prospect list, you can make huge progress with the above-noted six modes to drive your instruction-centered marketing messages.

Importance of Aligning Your Messages and Marketplace Interactions

One final point on instruction-centered marketing, or whatever marketing approach your firm chooses to employ, involves the importance of everyone "singing-out-of-the-same-hymnal" when it comes to marketplace interactions. Far too often when a firm is taking a non-strategic approach to attracting external opportunities, there is no cohesive marketing-related message conveyed by its professionals. The result is mush. Engaging in the exercises described in Chapter 4 will be a helpful first step to creating consistency within your firm.

Chapter 7 References

[i]Holmes, Chet. *The Ultimate Sales Machine—Turbocharge Your Business with Relentless Focus on 12 Key Strategies*. Penguin Group (USA) Inc., New York, NY, 2007. Pages 60-61

[ii]Ibid. Page 64

[iii]Ibid. Page 63

[iv]Ibid. Page 64

[v]Ibid. Page 64

[vi]See relevant citations in Chapter 5.

[vii]Schultz, Mike; Doerr, John E.; and Fredericksen, Lee W., PhD—and the RAIN Group, LLC. *Professional Services Marketing—How the Best Firms Build Premier Brands, Thriving Lead Generation Engines, and Cultures of Business*

Development Success. John Wiley & Sons, Inc., Hoboken, NJ, 2009 and 2013. Page 242

[viii]Ibid. Pages 243 and 246

[ix]Pulizzi, Joe. *Epic Content Marketing—How to Tell a Different Story, Break Through the Clutter, and Win More Customers By Marketing Less.* McGraw-Hill Education Books/Joe Pulizzi, Columbus, OH, 2014. Pages 4-6, 9-10, 30, 47

[x]Op. cit. Schultz, Doerr, and Fredericksen. Pages 183, 190-191, 193

[xi]Op. cit. Holmes. Pages 65-66, and 74

[xii]Abraham, Jay. *Money-making Secrets of Marketing Genius Jay Abraham and Other Marketing Wizards.* Abraham Publishing Group, Inc., Rolling Hills Estates, CA 1993, 1994. Page 112

[xiii]Frederiksen, Lee W., PhD; McVey, Sean T.; Montgomery, Sylvia; and Taylor, Aaron. *Online Marketing for Professional Services.* Hinge Research Institute, Reston, VA, 2012. Pages 37-42

[xiv]Frederiksen, Lee W. PhD.; Taylor, Aaron, E. *Spiraling Up—How to Create a High Growth, High Value Professional Services Firm.* Hinge Research Institute, Reston, VA, 2010. Page 92

CHAPTER 8

PROACTIVELY SET INITIAL MEETINGS—BEST BUYER PROSPECTS

This is a chapter that may give some of you the heebie-jeebies, proactively setting meetings with Best Buyer prospects. Let me assure you that I'm as introverted as the rest of you CPAs, and this is something I've had to learn to do, and pretty effectively. If it's been a while since I've reached out to prospects for meetings, I can get the jitters, and find better things to do with my time first, like tidy up my desk or surf the web, before finally picking up the phone to connect with them.

Another aspect that periodically distressed me was, here I was, a guy at the highest strata of earnings for CPA firm partners, essentially telemarketing to set appointments with target clientele. I'd think to myself, "Isn't there *someone else* I could offload this process to?" I'd use various call-centers from time to time, but their inconsistencies were problematic. Particularly where travel was involved to visit with prospects. I'd fly-off to New York or Philadelphia, or drive up to Chicago, only to find I'm meeting with some very junior person with little authority or interest in meeting, or worse, the planned attendee was a no-show for our scheduled appointment. Call centers often burned through prospect leads like dry kindling as well. Since I was frequently involved in starting new service areas, and *had to start showing results quickly*, I ultimately had to take charge of setting meetings and selling, or deal with unpleasant scrutiny from the powers that be.

I eventually concluded:

- No call center personnel on planet earth could describe the purpose of our needing to meet with a sophisticated prospective Best Buyer better than me and my teammates.

- Most executive-level Best Buyer personnel would likely perceive it unfavorably that I was too lazy, arrogant, busy, uncourageous—whatever—to pick up the phone and call them myself.

When you think about it, hopefully no one can articulate why you want to meet with a high-value prospect better than you can, and presumably to the extent you're needing or wanting to grow your firm's topline, you've got ample time to set-up your own meetings as well. What finally cleared my conscious about cold calling Best Buyer prospects, though, was an article I came across in *Fortune Magazine* about current Florida Governor Rick Scott.

I first became acquainted with who Rick Scott is several years ago, through meetings with professionals from his family office private equity firm in Connecticut. Background-wise, Governor Scott attended a commuter college in Missouri, and received a law degree from Southern Methodist University. Later, he served in the U.S. Navy before starting his law career at the Dallas firm Johnson & Swanson. In 1987, he co-founded Columbia Hospital Corporation, subsequently merging it with Hospital Corporation of America in 1989 to form Columbia/HCA, which later became the largest for-profit hospital in the U.S..

Politically, Scott first ran for Governor of Florida in 2010, defeating Bill McCollum in the Republican primary, and Democratic nominee

Alex Sink in the general election. In 2014 he won re-election against former Republican Florida Governor, turned Democrat, Charlie Crist.[i] You'd probably say that Rick Scott is a pretty important guy who has a lot on his plate.

Excerpts from the January 2012 *Fortune Magazine* piece, "Rick Scott, the Florida Governor, doesn't look like a governor. Standing behind the desk in his office, shifting his weight with nervous energy, he looks like a telemarketer. The former healthcare tycoon is wearing a wireless headset on his narrow bald pate and a white work shirt with his name stitched across the breast. He quickly scans a call sheet, bends down to tap out a phone number, then straightens up and waits."

"'Hi, Jeff,' Scott says unsteadily to the telecom executive on the other end of the line. 'This is Governor Rick Scott. How are you doing?'

"Scott has let me observe this weekly ritual. He spends an hour cold-calling CEOs, taking their temperature, but also trying to persuade them to open up shop or expand further in the Sunshine State. Scott wants those employers. With enough of them, he's sure he can shake Florida's economic malaise.

"Nobody knows for sure how to pull off the economic turnaround the new governor is aiming for, and Scott, 59, is an unlikely figure to lead the charge. He's never held elected office, he is trying to bring his aggressive style to the governorship."[ii]

Take a moment to think about what you just read in the last several paragraphs. *The governor of the third most populous state in the U.S. cold calls businesses to locate and/or expand in Florida.* The full *Fortune* article describes Governor Scott as being an introvert. With Governor Scott, *we all have* a prominent role model to ditch the excuse that we are too busy, highly-paid, shy, or important to pick up the phone or otherwise make appointments with Best Buyer prospects.

To the extent you still have some phobia about picking up that device invented by Alexander Graham Bell in 1876 to meet with Best Buyer prospect clients, I'd invite you to revisit Chapter 1 (Your Mindset), to learn how to overcome limiting beliefs and the fears or failure or rejection.

Contacts for Appointments

Here we go, getting in front of your Best Buyer prospects. This is an approach I've used and taught my teammates to employ, with excellent results.

I'm presuming that prior to reaching out to these prospective clientele, you and your firm have softened the market by conducting a couple of months of instruction-centered marketing mailers and emails to your Best Buyer 100 prospects (each month would include two to three snail mail or email contacts to the individuals you intend to ultimately meet). Hopefully, after such marketing tactics, each Best Buyer will have at least some familiarity with your firm's name, and perhaps, who you are too.

The first suggestion I'd make is that you schedule specific days to conduct out-of-office meetings with Best Buyer prospects. I know what you're thinking—don't you want to take into account what these prospects have availability-wise? Sure. But you need to start somewhere, and by your scheduling exact dates for these meetings on your calendar, it draws purpose to those timeframes, and you expectantly won't get mired-down in other activities because you've staked-out meeting days. Ditto for your Best Buyer prospects. With advance planning on your part, they conceivably won't be overscheduled for your proposed meeting dates, either. If you're striving to build a practice with Best Buyers located in another part of the country, where you need to book air travel and hotels, you'll want to plan far enough in advance to keep travel costs as affordable as possible.

Next, I recommend starting out with a phone call to the person you want to meet with. Since this is probably something that's new to you, I'd suggest you write down a script of your message, and rehearse what you intend to say so it has an air of being natural before commencing your calls. You'll want to include references in your script to:

- Who your firm and you are

- If someone referred you to them, who that was

- The instruction-centered marketing data the Best Buyer has presumably seen

- Why you want to meet

- How much time you'll take

- Your date and time options

There is an excellent chance you'll get your prospect's voice-mail when you call, so plan on leaving your scripted message for them. Here is an example script for that purpose, assuming you're calling on Terry at QRS Manufacturing, a Best Buyer prospect.

Hi Terry! My name is John Smith and I'm one of the senior partners in the manufacturing practice at XYZ, LLP in Los Angeles, the accounting and advisory firm. I received your name from one of our clients, Ralph Jones at ABC Industries in Pasadena. Over the past couple months, we've sent your way several of our white papers about "Adverse Trends Impacting California Manufacturers, and How to Prosper in Any Environment." My teammate Mary Williams and I were hoping to get on your schedule for 30-minutes or so on either Tuesday, April 3, or Wednesday April 4, to understand more about QRS Manufacturing's focus, and to share with you some of the manufacturing-related issues we've observed in the marketplace, as well as how our clients have addressed them. When you have an opportunity today, please contact me at 800-123-4567. I'll send you a short email too. Thanks much, Terry.

Some might think that's a long message. It will take you less than a minute to convey, *and* it gets across who you are, what you want, and what they might gain from the time investment.

Others don't believe in leaving voice-mail messages involving sales or marketing-related matters. That's nonsense. With the difficulty of actually catching someone live, you'll be making fruitless calls for an eternity if you're averse to leaving a short message.

As noted, you promised to send a short email too about the appointment. Plan on doing so within moments of your voice message. Here's what it could look like:

Email Subject:

Quick Meeting at QRS Manufacturing on Tuesday April 3, or Wednesday April 4

Message:

Dear Terry:

I just left you a voice mail message a few moments ago as well.

My name is John Smith and I'm one of the senior partners in the manufacturing practice at XYZ, LLP in Los Angeles, the accounting and advisory firm. I received your name from one of our clients, Ralph Jones at ABC Industries in Pasadena, and he suggested we connect.

Over the past couple months, we've sent several of our white papers on "Adverse Trends Impacting California Manufacturers, and How to Prosper in Any Environment." My teammate Mary Williams and I were hoping to get on your schedule for 30-minutes or so on either Tuesday April 3, or Wednesday April 4, to understand more about QRS Manufacturing's focus, and to share with you some of the industry-related issues we've observed in the marketplace, as well as how our clients have addressed them.

When you have an opportunity today, please let me know what time would work with you. If more convenient, please feel free to contact me at 800-123-4567.

Thanks in advance for your response Terry!

Warmly,

John Smith, CPA, Partner

Again, short and sweet.

What's the likelihood of hearing back from Terry right away? Slim odds of that happening, unless Ralph Jones at ABC Industries is a real pal, Terry is experiencing lots of pain in his manufacturing company and his current advisor is AWOL, or he's one of these rare folks that returns all calls and emails in a timely fashion.

What do you do then, when there's no response with your initial request? Wait forty-eight hours and repeat both your voice mail and email contacts in a similar way.

Everyone's Busy, and They Won't Return My Calls or Emails!

You might be thinking, I'm somewhat Pollyanna to believe that all your Best Buyer prospects will respond to your first or second meeting requests, because you've tried doing stuff like this before. All I can say is, yes, everyone IS busy, and their attention is certainly splintered. That doesn't mean you can't get an affirmative reply relatively quickly on your meeting request. Through the years, I've spoken with call centers that might make six, eight, ten rounds of calls to set appointments, sometimes leaving follow-up messages and sometimes not, because they didn't want to bother the prospect. Eventually, they give-up in frustration, after burning through mountains of prospect opportunities, and your money, in the process. I'd like to share with you a technique I learned from Dan Fensin, the late managing partner of Blackman, Kallick Bartelstein, LLP in Chicago, which significantly shortens this process and gets great results, too.

Mr. Fensin was the long-time MP of Blackman Kallick. A fun guy with a stereotypical Chicago dialect and a practical leadership style. In the late 1990s and early 2000s BKB was a client of mine for various specialty tax services, and I interacted with Dan and other Blackman partners regularly. When I'd be out of the office and Mr. Fensin would call and leave me a voice mail message, he'd always conclude it with, "Patrick, I'd appreciate the courtesy of a response."

Now during my 36-year career I'd *always* return client, co-worker, and prospect calls with hyper speed. However, Dan's requesting the "courtesy of a response" really made an impression, a deep neural pathway in my brain. What I later discovered was that by discretely using such phrase, I could *dramatically improve* upon getting most folks to respond to meeting requests affirmatively, or just about any other circumstance where they were tardy in replying.

Let's pretend your second set of calls and emails go unanswered, what should you do? After twenty-four to forty-eight hours from your last attempt, place a third call, followed by an email. Here's the call's content script:

Hey Terry, this is John Smith, the senior partner at XYZ, LLP here in Los Angeles. I had reached out a couple times each via e-mail and voice mail about getting on your calendar for 30-minutes or so on either April 3rd or 4th with my colleague Mary Williams.

Terry, as you know, it can be challenging to put together an out-of-town travel schedule and weekly meeting calendar, so when you have an opportunity today, I'd appreciate the courtesy of a response.

Thanks and have a great day!

Follow it up immediately with a similarly-structured email:

Email Subject:

Fwd. Follow-up, Quick Meeting at QRS Manufacturing on Tuesday April 3rd or Wednesday April 4th

Message:

Dear Terry:

I just left you a voice mail message a few moments ago.

During the week, I've reached out a couple times via phone and email about my teammate Mary Williams and I getting on your schedule for 30-minutes or so on either Tuesday April 3rd or Wednesday April 4th (please see the original e-mail message below).

As you know, it can be challenging to put together a/an _____ (fill-in the blank), so when you have an opportunity today, I'd appreciate the courtesy of a response.

Thanks much!

John Smith

How effective is this? It is *hugely effective* in getting individuals to respond to you. More than 95 percent effective. Why? My sense is that most folks genuinely don't want to be discourteous, and you're gently reminding them that ignoring someone's meeting requests are, well, impolite. Most of those responding do actually agree to meet, unless they really are out-of-town or there's something else they can't reschedule. What I've found though, is if they truly are unavailable, they'll often find someone of value to meet with you.

I've taught this approach to teammates too, those that had the hutzpah to actually use it, would get the same 95-percent plus response rate.

No doubt, some will say, "Wow, *that's **way** too assertive* for me." Use whatever approach you like, just don't complain when you're not getting in front of your Best Buyer prospects. In my case, I absolutely needed to fill my calendar with high-quality appointments, particularly with out-of-town travel costs, etc., so I used the approach often.

Some of my co-workers would only opt to simply email prospects, sans the phone call, and would, likewise, achieve poor outcomes. You really need to *utilize both modes* of contact. When you put them together, for whatever reason, prospects appear to be much more responsive. For those prospects who continue to be unresponsive, employing the courtesy of a response request seemingly corrals most of them.

A final matter to consider, once you've established contact with your Best Buyer prospect, involves breaking news. To help you keep in contact as developments arise, think about establishing Google Alerts for both the Best Buyer prospect company and all of its key executives. When news occurs, you'll be able to beat others to the punch with a congratulatory email or an inquiry about the event.

When Should You Give Up?

I'd like to share a personal story about my father, Raymond. My dad was a genuinely nice guy—quiet and somewhat docile. He worked at U.S. Steel's Gary Works. We all have seminal events in our lives. This, perhaps is mine—and it involves persistence.

As a kid, I loved baseball, especially the Chicago White Sox. The little league I played for in downtown Gary, Indiana, was called Elk's, and I played for a team sponsored by the city's mayor, A. Martin Katz. We were the Katz Kittens Sox, talk about an awful name. We had a won/loss record that matched our loser name—I think we finished the season at 1-19. We had no offense. We had no defense.

I was a pitcher for the Kittens. Notwithstanding our .050 winning percentage, I was an okay pitcher. I couldn't strike out the opposing side inning after inning though. *That was a problem.* Anytime an opposing batter made contact with the ball, he had a multi-base opportunity. If he'd hit a grounder to the shortstop, the shortstop would *maybe* field it. If he did, his throw to first was almost certainly going to be over the first baseman's head. By the time the first baseman got the ball, the runner was advancing for third base, and he'd rifle the ball towards third base, over the third baseman's head. So, the batter's grounder to short ended up being an inside the park homer.

This would happen inning after inning, game after game.

Once during one of these little league games, we were playing our opponent tight, but darn-it, some of their hitters started to make contact with the ball. Soon we were hopelessly behind. Disgusted, I feigned injury to put an end to my night's misery.

My pop was in the bleachers, and saw through my poor acting job. He was peeved, to put it nicely. During the entire ride home from the ballpark, he railed on my quitting, and that no matter what the outcome ultimately was, I'd better not do that quitting thing ever again. Now, although I have many faults as a person, giving-up isn't one of them. Dad would be proud.

Perseverance has been a godsend in building the units I've been involved in. I could tell story after story where grit ultimately made the difference in winning big engagements. I'll share a couple:

Several years ago, when we were building our alliances with CPA firms to perform specialty tax services on a fee-sharing approach, I had targeted a nice-sized firm in the deep-south to work with us. I grew up just outside Chicago, so culturally, I didn't exactly talk like those folks or have a lot in common with them, other than being a CPA.

I spoke with the managing partner of this southern firm, who punted me to another leadership team partner. I'd call this partner, and call this partner, and call this partner. He wouldn't respond (this is before I learned about the magic phrase, "I'd appreciate the courtesy of the response"). I then started to track the number of my calls, 33, 34, 35. On the 36th call, I *finally* spoke with the designated partner to describe our alliance program. Apparently, their practice was part of a national firm's technical network, and the sponsoring firm had just stubbed-their-toe servicing an important client of this deep-south CPA firm. It was our in. Within a week, we had a meeting at the CPA firm's headquarters, and during our visit, we were engaged for our first project.

In subsequent years, we were hired on nearly 100 projects with this accountancy group. My guess is that had we given up after just a handful of calls, because we perceived that they weren't interested, those seven-figure fees we ultimately derived from that CPA firm, would have never materialized.

Another circumstance of note happened with a New York City-based private equity group. This shop had more than $1 billion in committed capital. During our first meeting, they told us they *loved* their Big Four provider. At the conclusion of our session, their key executive said, "It was great to meet you guys. Have a nice life!"

An awesome thing about business is that circumstances change, often for the good. About a year after this meeting, there was a change in the PE firm's executive team, and the guy that gave us the bum's rush was gone. We scheduled a meeting with the new guy, and he liked what we had to say. Although they were going to continue using their Big Four provider on major investments, they said they would give us a shot at add-on deals and smaller platform transactions.

Long story short, they were thrilled with our team, and our data-analytics approach. One deal became ten, ten became twenty. Ultimately, they became an essential client of our group, generating substantial annual fees. The moral of the story is, a not now doesn't always mean not ever.

Perseverance in the face of rejection or when being ignored, is one of the keys to getting meetings and growing your firm in the long-term.

So when do you give up? *Never!*

Perhaps there are *some* cases when you can consider giving up. When you're threatened with a restraining order to stop calling, would be an example. The prospect goes out of business, or you've retired from the profession are a couple others.

If the prospect asks you to back off, then back off. But as the above stories note, to the extent you persist, good things generally happen. Quit, and they typically don't. As Wayne Gretzky, arguably the greatest hockey player ever would say, "You always miss 100 percent of the shots you don't take."

As discussed in Chapter 7, having a live session with your Best Buyer prospect is truly critical, and reaching out to set an appointment is the precursor to meeting eyeball-to-eyeball. In-person meetings are one of the few opportunities to have a prospect's undivided attention. *That's why they're musts.* In a study of the fastest growing professional services firms in the U.S., "personal visits to prospects" was delineated as one of the preferred marketing modes of high-growth firms versus their below-average and average-growth compatriots.[iii] So, do what those successful firms do!

Chapter 8 References

[i]http://en.wikipedia.org/wiki/Rick_Scott

[ii]Newmyer, Tory. "The Education of Florida Governor Rick Scott." *Fortune Magazine*, January 16, 2012.

[iii]Frederiksen, Lee W. PhD.; Taylor, Aaron, E. *Spiraling Up—How to Create a High Growth, High Value Professional Services Firm*. Hinge Research Institute, Reston, VA, 2010. Page 92

CHAPTER 9

INITIAL MEETINGS AND SALES PROCESSES

You've identified your Best Buyer prospects, softened the market with instruction-centered content, and set up a live meeting. In this chapter, we'll first describe specific aspects of the sales process for accounting-related professional services, and then tailor it for your initial meeting with a Best Buyer.

Meeting with a potential client is a dynamic encounter. Irrespective of how we chart this, there will *always* be nuances, simply because no two people or prospect sessions are identical. These are guidelines for your consideration.

The I^5—Close Approach

The I^5—Close Approach involves six discrete parts to sales-related practices in the professional services arena. Obviously, these chunks have a way of blending together. Chapter 10 addresses a methodology for more complex proposal settings. The process is summarized in the model below:

The I⁵—Close Approach Model

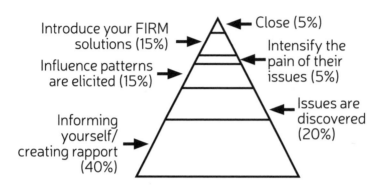

Introduce your FIRM solutions (15%) →
← Close (5%)

Influence patterns are elicited (15%) →
← Intensify the pain of their issues (5%)

← Issues are discovered (20%)

Informing yourself/ creating rapport (40%) →

Following is a more detailed description of the elements:

Informing yourself and creating rapport: We discussed practices helpful in creating compelling rapport within Chapter 2. Similarly, other skills discussed in Chapter 2, such as listening to win, the power of quality questions, magic words and basic language patterns, will have a *huge* positive impact on informing yourself and building an even deeper connection, and are worth reviewing too. Incredibly, it's estimated that 40 percent of success in sales-related settings is attributable to this portion of the sales process.[i]

Informing yourself seems to be one of the ABCs of going into a prospect session, but I've seen *far* too many instances where that important step was ignored. Today, there is ample data available about your Best Buyer via normal Internet searches, publicly-available regulatory filings, social media sites (particularly LinkedIn for executives), and discussions with others within the prospect's industry. There are few secrets out there. Best Buyers often can sense when you've done a perfunctory job getting ready for them versus having conducted your homework.

An indicator of preparation typically involves the questions your teammates and you raise in your initial Best Buyer meeting. In

Power Questions, the authors Andrew Sobel and Jerold Panas relay a story about an interview they conducted with a high-powered CEO of a $12-billion Chicago-based company. They inquired, "What most impresses you when you meet with someone who is trying to win your business? What builds trust and credibility?"[ii] The exec thought for a moment, considered service providers his company used again and again, and that he viewed as part of his inner circle of trusted advisors. He responded, "I can always tell how experienced and insightful a prospective consultant, banker, or lawyer is by the quality of the questions asked, and how intently they listen. That's how simple it is."[iii]

The authors' research, which included hundreds of business-leader interviews, points to the importance of questions, and how the inquirer listens, as important steps in building a successful new relationship. In fact, they've concluded that, "Good questions are far more powerful than answers."[iv]

So, if excellent questions are an indication of your pre-meeting diligence and professional skills, doesn't it then make sense to carve-out time beforehand to map-out relevant questions for your Best Buyer?

Initial meetings can be a little uncomfortable at first. An approach I've often used to get the ball rolling is to start with a statement that lets prospects know that we've done our homework—while referring to a stack of documents brought to the meeting. Next, I'll state, "Obviously, what you read about a company, and what happens at the firm in real life can be quite different." I'd then ask the prospect to talk about the company from their point of view, and to tell us a little about their own background. As mentioned in Chapter 2, most people *love* to talk about their company and themselves, so prepare to sit back, listen and take notes. Show you're paying attention, but *don't interrupt them*. You're getting informed and building rapport.

Other effective initial meeting questions could include:

- You've certainly built an incredibly successful _____ (e.g., career, company, reputation, etc.). How did you get started in the _____ ?

- With the work we're involved with in the _____ (e.g., banking, agricultural, etc.) industry, we've been wrapping our heads around _____ (name the issues the clients in your industry have been mentioning or struggling with). How do you think about those issues?

- There are some great companies in _____ (name either your local industry or geographic area, like the Oklahoma independent energy sector or the western Chicago suburbs). Who are some of the businesses (or people) you most admire?

Again, advance preparation is *essential*, along with asking quality initial questions in order to be both informed and build rapport.

Issues are discovered: During your initial research and discussions, telltale concerns may crop-up. Once you've allowed your Best Buyer prospect to fully answer your preliminary questions (while you've diligently listened and taken notes), you can ask them, "Could you rewind the tape to a few minutes ago? You mentioned having some challenges with _____ . I'm wondering if you could tell us more about that?" In other words, it's *totally* appropriate to request the prospective client to elaborate more on their issues, once you've let them fully respond to your initial information-related inquiries. Don't assume you can mind read the prospect, however, don't behave like the embodiment of Google Search either—ready to show the prospect how smart you are with an answer to their problem. Prod by asking if they can tell you more about it, so you fully understand the extent of their issue.

Okay, what if the Best Buyer is reticent about articulating their concerns. How can you tease them out? Elegantly framed questions can help uncover prospect business problems. Here are a few you can use as models:

- "Wow, it seems like you've got a lot of things going on. I'm curious, are there any aspects of your work-related activities that you'd love to delve into more, or, alternatively, spend less time on?"

- Depending on their answer to the preceding query, you can pose the follow-up question, "What prevents you from being able to do that?"

- "You mentioned _____ (their specific problem) as being an issue for you. Is this a petty annoyance or something that needs to get fixed soon?"

- "Earlier, you noted you've work with XYZ CPAs for several years. Presumably all's been well, but, I'm wondering, if you had a magic wand and could improve anything about your experience with XYZ, what would that be?" Remember, to the extent they say something useful, ask, "Could you please tell me more about that?" Recall from Chapter 2, that the word *but* negates the portion of the sentence that precedes it, so presumably all is not well.

- "What's missing in your relationship with XYZ?"

- "You indicated _____ has been a continuing issue. How much is this costing you (or, how much has this cost you up till now)?"

- "Is this problem with _____ impacting others in your department, or are other aspects of your business being adversely affected by this issue?"[v]

Again, you're exploring to discover and understand their specific business-related issues.

Are there poor issue-discovery questions? According to authors Sobel and Panas, there are. They relay a story of a CEO of North American operations of a multinational public company. This CEO notes he's been called on by the most sophisticated sales professionals in the country, "But recently, threw a salesperson out of his office for asking *the* question. What keeps you up at night?" The CEO described the question as, "Overused. Clichéd. Stale. And worst of all, lazy. I hate lazy salespeople the executive noted."[vi] I'd second that CEO's view. I've heard other professionals blurt-out that inquiry in meetings, and came close to choking.

How important is this discovery of issues segment to being successful in sales settings? One thought leader predicts it's in the 20-percent range.[vii] Presumably, this detective work is where you can begin to differentiate your firm, and find ways to trigger a Best Buyer prospect to consider changing service providers.

Influence patterns are elicited: In the language-based psychology subfield, NLP, there is a concept called meta-programs. Most of us are bombarded by information, communications, and other data. Much of this flies right past us unnoticed. Our meta-programs act as an opening or screen in communications, with messages that fit within the opening having an impact, or resonating with us. Those that don't fit, are just filtered-out.[viii]

There are two broad categories of meta-programs, motivation traits and decision traits, and within those two classes, roughly fourteen individual types of meta-programs. We will only address four, a handful that will benefit you in professional services sales settings. To the extent that you have a passion to dig deeper into the other meta-program types, there are numerous books and reference tools available.[ix]

Meta-programs act as a shortcut in our thinking process. They effect where individuals place their attention, what they respond to, and what motivates them. In essence, they are an individual's preferred way of being communicated to. These patterns operate unconsciously, in the background, just like computer software. In some cases, you can pick-up on Best Buyers' meta-programs by listening to them speak. I've also found that by simply asking a few questions, you can elicit their most important traits. Note, meta-programs can, and do, shift based on the context. For example, the meta-programs a person operates under in sales settings at work may be entirely different from their processes at home.

Let's look at the first, and most important meta-program . . .

Criteria

Criteria is a term that encompasses the values that are important to someone in a particular context. They are analogous to beliefs in that they help a person decide what is right or wrong and good or bad. Criteria are *extraordinary motivators and drivers of behavior*, and are frequently used by individuals to evaluate themselves and others.

You'll often see that a person's criteria are represented by a single word or phrase, and often they are nominalizations (see Chapter 2's discussion). Time after time, I've seen these criteria words produce a physical and/or emotional reaction in someone I'm speaking with. They are their hot buttons. People ascribe their own meaning to such hot buttons within a context.[x]

What's really unique, is that you may never need to actually know your prospects' definition of their criteria, although it is helpful. In sales settings, it's imperative that you simply find out how they describe something they view as important or are excited about.[xi]

"Criteria can be captured by asking questions such as:

- What's important to you in _____ ?

- What counts in _____ ?

- What would you like there to be in a _____ ?"[xii]

The way I'll work this in during CPA-related sales settings is to tee up the question this way: "Obviously, you've worked with other advisors or CPAs up until now. I'm curious, when you work with professionals like us (normally I'll point to myself or tap myself on the chest), what's important to you from a client standpoint?"

When you ask that, many prospects will say that it's a great question, because *no one ever asks it*. When they do respond, they'll often use one or two-word replies, in list format, and say things like:

- Responsiveness

- Timeliness

- Creativity

- Accuracy

When they are answering your question, it's critical to copy down *exactly* what they say, **not** some word that has a similar meaning. You can probe to discern what some of these criteria actually mean. You might say, for example, "Thank you, that's *really* helpful. You know, responsiveness can mean a lot of different things to different people, what does it mean to you?" Often, they'll give you a clarifying example, describe what their specific rules for responsive performance are, or tell you about how the current advisor blundered in the area of responsiveness.

Many believe they can paraphrase similar criteria words back to a prospect to give them the impression they understand them, and can help them. Richard Bandler and John LaValle's book *Persuasion Engineering*, instead advocates "parrot phrasing." Parrot phrasing means, "Delivering back exactly and precisely what you hear and see, the hand demonstrations (i.e., movements), and everything that's useful to the process."[xiii]

Many of you might think that if you parrot phrase, the prospect will pick-up on what you're doing and be annoyed. Most people are so *unperceptive* that they likely won't even remember you asked the criteria question to begin with. To the extent that you weave in their parrot-phrased criteria (i.e., of what's important in a professional services provider) in your proposal or in subsequent one-on-one sales presentations, you'll have an important and persuasive leg-up.

From an ethics standpoint, if you're saying that you can deliver on the articulated criteria, you better be able to! Remember, bad karma strikes those who use techniques that are deceptive or inappropriate.

Let's move to our second important meta-program . . .

Direction

The direction meta-program describes "how people maintain motivation." Is their motivation driven by going for what they want, or, do they focus on what to avoid and what they don't want? Direction responses are sorted into two broad categories:

- **Towards:** "People with a towards pattern stay focused on their goal. They are generally motivated to have, get, achieve, or attain. They tend to be good at concentrating on key priorities."[xiv]

- **Away-from:** "When individuals are principally away-from, they easily recognize what should be avoided or shouldn't happen." Individuals with an away-from strategy are compelled to respond to negative situations.[xv]

The distribution for the direction meta-program is roughly 40 percent toward, 40 percent away-from and 20 percent who are equally toward and away-from.[xvi]

A good way to pick-out an individual's direction meta-program is by simply listening to them. Do they discuss items that they want to gain, achieve, get, or have, or describe situations to be avoided or problems? You can also tease-out a direction meta-program by asking questions related to their criteria, which you elicited in the previous section, including:

- "Why is having that (criteria item) important to you?"

- "What will having _____ do for you?"

- "What's important about _____ ?"[xvii]

How do you influence someone with a toward or away-from direction strategy? For those who are mainly toward, emphasize what they will attain, get, have, or achieve by _____ _____ . In contrast, for those with away-from strategies, indicate how they will be able to avoid, not have, exclude, or move-away-from _____ by doing _____ .[xviii]

A CPA-services sales-related example demonstrating both the criteria and direction meta-programs involved a northern California-based technology company that had recently engaged in a public stock offering. The company was looking for assistance on tax provision calculations, tax footnote disclosures, federal and state tax return preparation help, foreign structuring consulting, and various other projects. When we probed the tax director, we learned his principal criteria for working with a professional services provider was responsiveness. Probing responsiveness, we discerned the current international firm advisor would take days, or sometime a week, to return phone calls. The tax director told us, "He didn't want to wait around for a week to get his calls returned." Clearly, an away-from pattern.

When we met with him a few days later to highlight our proposal, you can be sure of one of our key discussion points, can't you? We discussed how our clients appreciate the responsiveness we show by returning all calls within 24-hours, often less—and how our clients know they won't wait around for a week to discuss their key concerns and get answers.

Like criteria, the direction meta-program can shift depending on context, so pay particular attention to responses in your professional sales-setting discussions.

Source

The next overall meta-program addresses how someone makes a decision. The source meta-program concentrates on whether a person is influenced more by external sources, such as being based on feedback from bosses, customers and co-workers, or from their own internal standards or beliefs—they just knew the client was happy, they did a good job, or that this was the right decision. Individuals tend to fall into one of two source categories in particular contexts:

- **Internal:** Those with principally an internal strategy provide their own self-motivation, make their own decisions about things, and are less influenced by the views or opinions of others. They have challenges buying into others' opinions and outside direction. When they get negative feedback on projects they personally believe they've succeeded at, they'll likely

191

question the views and wisdom of the person doling out the criticism. They may gather data from outsiders, but they make decisions about its accuracy and propriety, and make a final choice personally.[xix]

- **External:** Those with a high external meta-program trait, deeply value the opinions and direction of others. "If they do not get feedback at work, for example, they may not know how well they are performing." In sales scenarios, references, case studies, and the like are valuable influencers.[xx]

It is estimated that roughly 40 percent of individuals are mainly external, 40 percent mainly internal, and 20 percent equally external and internal in a particular context.[xxi]

Questions to ask to elicit one's source meta-program include:[xxii]

- "How do you know that you've done well at _____ ?"

- "How would you react to comments from _____ (peers, your advisors, regulators, etc.) in (a specific context)?"

- "Who do you involve in the process, when you make a decision about _____ ?"

In response to such questions, "Individuals with principally internal traits might:

- Decide personally, or they know themselves.

- Evaluate _____ based on their own benchmarks.

- Pushback when someone tells them what to do involving _____ ."[xxii]

"Those with a more dominant external trait might:

- Use other people or external sources of data to play a key role, decide, or judge for them.

- Need to compare their views with what _____ has to say.

- Have _____ tell them that our work was _____ ."[xxiv]

How do you influence someone with a principal internal trait? In general, the following communications can be effective at persuading a dominant internal individual:

- What do *they* know! Only you can decide if _____ is right for you.

- *You're* the boss. You know it's up to you to _____ .

- What do you think about _____ ?

- You might want to consider _____ .

- I'd invite you to consider _____ .

- A suggestion for you to think about is _____ .[xxv]

Those with a principally external source meta-program trait are likely to be influenced by language such as:

- The feedback you'll get about _____ will surely be _____ .

- The approval you'll get from your _____ will be excellent!

- Others will notice just how _____ .

- _____ thinks it's a great idea for you to _____ .[xxvi]

In addition to couching messages in the above-noted way, those with external traits appreciate receiving references of other clients.

Let's shift our attention to the final meta-program filter we'll highlight . . .

Scope

The scope meta-program deals with the amount or type of information a person handles well or processes best (i.e., the "chunk size"). Concerning scope, individuals typically fall into one of two categories:

- **"Specific:** People with a specific trait handle small pieces of information better." They enjoy getting into the minutia, and discussing projects in a step-by-step fashion. They may have difficulty getting a feel for the overview, or a big picture.[xxvii]

- **"General:** Those with a general trait prefer to work on the overview or at a conceptual level. These individuals may present ideas in a random order, jumping around from item to item." They may get bored and lose interest when you delve into details.[xxviii]

The approximate distribution of this trait is: 60 percent general, 15 percent specific, and 25 percent those equally affected by a general and specific approach.[xxix]

In NLP training literature, there are no explicit questions to identify specific versus general traits, you merely need to listen to a person's speech. In many cases, executives you're speaking with will guide you towards their preference. Do they want to get into the nitty-gritty for example, or do they want the big picture? Time-limits for a meeting might dictate the approach you'll have to use, as well. To the extent you'd like to discern a preferred meeting scope approach with a prospect, a couple elegant questions might include:

- "Given what we've set forth in our proposal, and thinking about the value to you, can you say something about what you'd like to see more of or less of."[xxx]

- "We had planned to cover the following areas _____ . What parts will be the most valuable for us to emphasize?"[xxxi]

Having discerned your Best Buyer's influence patterns, we'll continue with the next segment of the I^5- Close Approach by learning how to . . .

Intensify the pain of their issues: Through the first two steps of the I^5-Close Approach you've gained a significant amount knowledge about the Best Buyer, as well as issues relating to their professional services provider. You may have learned about other delivery-related challenges too via eliciting their criteria and direction meta-programs. Your firm's probing-through the Best Buyer's collective historical "issues" is outstanding, now getting them to fully appreciate the painful consequences of these issues both presently, and in the future, is where an indecisive prospect can get flipped towards changing firms.

As described in Chapters 5 and 7, there are meaningful percentages of prospects that are persuadable for shifting all, or a portion of their professional services spends to your firm and you. Associating them to their issues is an effective way to break the inertia of keeping with their status-quo CPA. The principal means of doing so involves restating their previously-noted issues, followed by querying about what the consequence are now or will be down-the-road. Consequences can include missed opportunities, financial costs, time constraints, or pretty much any other work-related discomfort you've identified.

You can verbally pile-on their angst, and intensify the pain of their issues, by modeling some of the following statement/question combinations:

- "You've stated how the XYZ accounting firm regularly misses your agreed-upon deadlines. What's that going to cost you when you break your lender's covenants for submitting the audited financials late?"

- "You said that if you could wave a magic wand and improve anything about your experience with XYZ, that you'd substantially increase the involvement of their partners and higher-level professionals. With the amount of change in your industry, how much are you missing out on now and in the future without having such a key advisor by your side?"

- "You mentioned that XYZ's tax practice doesn't have any international tax professionals involved in your engagement, even though 25 percent of your operations are in Europe. With the complexity in cross-border planning, coupled with all the transfer pricing landmines out there, how are you coping with the millions in exposure potential or lost tax savings?"

- "You indicated that responsiveness has been a problem. I'm sure that's frustrating, you probably waste a lot of time too, just waiting and waiting. What's going to happen when you really need an answer fast and it causes you to miss a deadline?"

- "You joked that every year it seems as if XYZ unloads a school bus full of kids at the start of your audit. How much time do you think you'll expend again this next cycle on such an unexperienced crew?"

Again, let your education from the client and professional creativity lead you. Now it's time for you and your firm to ...

Introduce your FIRM solutions: In the four prior steps you've developed rapport and informed yourself about the Best Buyer, discovered their issues, learned how to best influence them language-wise, and intensified the discomfort of their existing service-related issues. By introducing your FIRM solutions, you're using social proof to vividly demonstrate how you've saved money or time and/or mitigated risk, using business examples that look just like the type of situations that they are facing now.

As discussed in Chapter 3, many prospects don't have a complete understanding of complex accounting, tax, and consulting issues and how to resolve them. Consequently, that is why having an excellent inventory of client case studies, and testimonials can be so *valuable* in convincing prospects of your firm's capability to solve problems and add value.

Case studies should be used to talk through an analogous problem, or circumstance with your prospect, versus being sent to them electronically or via mail to figure out on their own. They should be brief enough to get the key issue points across, however, not so long they lapse into a coma. Case studies involving data analytics, like the one in Chapter 3, had an impressive impact on private equity prospects that were frustrated with their CPA and transaction advisors who were unable to capture financial information surrounding their proposed investments. The approach toward crafting FIRM case studies was discussed in Chapter 6.

An elegant step to add in connection with introducing your FIRM solutions involves an NLP concept known as future pacing. Future pacing, coupled with FIRM solutions, involves suggesting that your Best Buyer step into the future and imagine what it will be like after having made the change in accounting service provider and availing the FIRM solution(s) you've proffered. So using the data-analytics case study from Chapter 3, you might suggest, "Imagine it's six months from today and you've just executed a letter-of-intent on a messy middle-market deal. But, instead of being frustrated, you're now able to confidently break down the target's profitability product-by-product line easily, because of availing XYZ's data-analytics approach. Can you see how much better this will be for your team and you?"

The basic format of future pacing is to imagine that it's _____ (sometime in the future), that you've made the change to _____ (something you do, or some solution you provide), and instead of being _____ (frustrated), you're are _____ (getting the wanted result). Can you see _____ (how much better, etc.) it will be for your company and you?

Some of you might perceive future pacing as being a little over-the-top. It's not a critical component to this professional services sales approach, nevertheless, some folks feel it is elegant and useful.

Let's move to the final segment of this approach . . .

Close: This unfortunately will be anticlimactic after the preceding steps of the sales process. When you've covered your bases on all the I⁵'s, closing often simply involves asking—asking to proceed on what your next pre-identified logical step is. Depending on the context of your meeting, the close might be:

- Setting up a follow-up meeting with one of your firm's experts where you've identified a painful issue. In other words, where you've found some wedge-issue.

- Providing some complimentary service such as a tax physical or SALT nexus review. Giving the Best Buyer a risk-free way to sample your firm's expertise.

- Proposing on a specific niche project, or a key segment of the relationship.

The key is to ask, *always* ask your Best Buyer for some next step, unless there is clearly no reason to continue pursuing the opportunity, such as discovering the prospect is not a Best Buyer or good fit for your firm. Remember the Wayne Gretzky quote, "You always miss 100 percent of the shots you don't take." You will be surprised how often asking will be embraced by the Best Buyer prospect.

Over the course of many tax co-sourcing initial meetings, we identified some wedge issue. In those cases, we'd be able to have a secondary session with a designated specialist. Alternatively, many prospects were open to having prior tax returns examined, on a complimentary basis for missed planning opportunities and the like.

Similarly, during many private equity meetings, prospects would discuss potential deals. Often, we would get into conversations with their executives about how we would approach that particular transaction, what we perceived the risk issues were, and how we might phase portions of the engagement to assure the target company was viable. When the PE prospect saw the depth of our knowledge, it created an opening. At the conclusion of our meeting, we'd request the opportunity to propose on the forthcoming deal, even though there was a go-to firm that the PE firm had historically been using. We'd note, "All it would involve is a little additional time for you to provide us data, if we lost out, we lost out. After all, that's what capitalism and the U.S. economy is based on, right?" In a number of instances, we'd get that shot, and, in a majority of those cases, we'd be selected. You have to ask!

What about objections? Isn't that part of the sales process? You bet it is. Nevertheless, one of the most effective means to deal with objections is to inoculate against them, just like a flu shot. Once you've had a few meetings with various Best Buyer prospects, you'll discover a handful of reasons that could cause your hopeful new client to pause or get cold feet. The most effective method of dealing with them in future meetings, is to then weave the common objections into your prospect conversation, and describe how they're simply non-issues.

If the notion of changing advisors seems daunting to some prospects, for example, you can find a way of weaving in, "From time-to-time a company contemplating a change in CPAs has some apprehension about the process. Largely because they've never done it before. With your decision to hire us, we'll reach out to the XYZ firm, and arrange to review prior year working papers and _____ . We even have letters drafted that you can use as a template to advise XYZ of your decision. Here is an example schematic of what the transition process looks like. We have a number of case studies that highlight just how smooth it is." Often, your best defense against common objections is a proactive offense to describe how it's not a concern.

What about objections you haven't planned for and didn't inoculate against? First, *never* disagree with your prospect about their objection. Acknowledge it. By doing so, aligning with their objection versus fighting against it, you deflate the objection's power somewhat. Next explain that other executives have raised the same question in the past and this is how you've handled it. Conclude by recognizing their issue, and reiterating how you've established safeguards to addresses it. If you perceive it would be helpful, and provide greater peace of mind, offer to have a reference contact them regarding how your firm and you have handled a matter like theirs previously.

Your Initial Meeting with a Best Buyer

In setting-up your Best Buyer meeting as modeled in Chapter 8, it was under the guise of understanding some facet of the Best Buyer's operations, and your firm or you sharing important content relevant to them. You *clearly* need to keep to that promised meeting script. Even though you only asked for 30-minutes or so, for scheduling purposes, plan on being there an hour. Here is a way to consider organizing for that very first session utilizing the I^5— Close Approach described above:

Informing yourself and developing rapport: All of the pre-meeting preparation steps described above apply. Know your Best Buyer prospect and the contemplated attendees as well as possible from your team's research. Build rapport utilizing the means described in Chapter 2. Start the substantive discussion with a question such as, "Our team has spent a fair amount of time reading about your firm and you. However, what you read and hear, versus what happens in real life can differ. Before we get into our part of the discussion, we'd love to hear a little about the company and yourself from your perspective." Sit back, listen, take notes, acknowledge, but *don't interrupt their flow*! Depending on how much time they've taken answering that overview question, you might be able to slide in a question or two to clarify their part of the dialogue.

Issues are discovered: As part of your pre-meeting study, you may have identified potential matters for discussion. Listening to them describe their business or themselves might raise a few other concerns too. As you present your instruction-centered content, be attentive to particular questions raised or body language from Best Buyer personnel that indicate you may have touched a hot button issue.

Influence patterns are elicited: Although it might seem a bit premature, it's not too early to discern their criteria pertaining to professionals. After you've presented your content, and perhaps answered a few questions related to it, it's the perfect time to say, "Obviously, you've worked with other advisors (or whomever their CPA firm is), up till now. I'm curious, when you work with professionals like us, what's important to you from a client standpoint?" Again, capture their words precisely! Once they've told you everything that's important to them, probe around for clarification. Listen closely to see if they're making references to how their current provider is dropping the ball on any of the important criteria, this is where it may be raised.

Intensify the pain of their issues: This doesn't necessarily have to be a *sky is falling* part of the meeting. Briefly recapping what their issue(s) are and how frustrating they can be (or the costs in terms of money, time, or risk), might be enough for an initial meeting.

Introduce your FIRM solutions: This does not need to be elaborate in a first session. If you've anticipated particular issues from your pre-meeting research and you have case studies with you that perfectly address their precise issues, you're amazing. It will be sufficient to say that one of your firm's professionals have handled circumstances exactly like theirs recently, assuming this has really happened, and that you'd like to have a follow-up meeting with this person and the potential client.

Close: Have something in mind as a close, and ask for it. If an issue has come up that one of your teammates has dealt with, say something to the effect of, "Considering this issue you've been grappling with, I'd like to have _____ from our firm have a complimentary meeting to discuss the matter further with your team and you. Does it make sense to find a mutually convenient time in the next _____?"

Follow-up: Although not articulated above, *there are always follow-up actions on your part.* If you've promised anything, do it immediately. Plan on penning a hand-written thank you card to all Best Buyer personnel that attended your meeting. No matter their level in the company—they gave you the gift of their time. I would recommend that you refer to some of the criteria referenced by the prospect in such a note, and how your firm delivers on them. Finally, get your follow-up meeting scheduled with your teammate and the Best Buyer prospect.

These are guidelines for your consideration. Meeting with a potential client is a dynamic encounter. There will *always* be nuances, simply because no two people or prospect sessions are identical.

Keeping track of data about each Best Buyer prospect can't be left to your memory or scraps of paper around your office. Appendix B contains a Short-form I[5]—Close Approach Document to capture critical background information as you advance each Best Buyer prospect forward to client status.

Let's move on to Chapter 10, and build on this material for more complex proposal settings.

Chapter 9 References

[i]Data was originally obtained via a presentation by Chet Holmes at Anthony Robbins' Business Mastery Seminar—and was purported to be research by his professionals; January 14, 2010. See also: Sears, Bob. *The Sales Process: The Seven Steps You Need To Know.* http://caryleadsgroup.net/the-sales-process, October 11, 2012.

[ii]Sobel, Andrew; Panas, Jerold. *Power Questions—Build Relationships, Win New Business, and Influence Others.* John Wiley & Sons, Inc., Hoboken, NJ, 2012. Page 3

[iii]Ibid. Page 3

[iv]Ibid. Page 4

[v]Ibid. Pages 186-188

[vi]Ibid. Page 63

[vii]Op. cit. Holmes.

[viii]O'Connor, Joseph and Seymour, John. *Introducing NLP—Neuro-Linguistic Programming*. Thorsons Publishing, San Francisco, CA, 1990. Page 149

[ix]Among the top books describing meta-programs are: *Words That Change Minds* by Shelle Rose Charvet; *Introducing NLP—Neuro-Linguistic Programming* by Joseph O'Connor and John Seymour; *Unlimited Power* by Anthony Robbins; and for a basic discussion, *Business NLP for Dummies* by Lynne Cooper.

[x]Charvet, Shelle Rose. *Words That Change Minds—Mastering the Language of Influence*. Kendall/Hunt Publishing Company, Dubuque, IA, 1997. Page 25

[xi]Ibid. Page 25

[xii]Ibid. Page 26

[xiii]Bandler Richard and LaValle, John. *Persuasion Engineering*. Meta Publications, Inc., Capitola, CA, 1996. Pages 64-65

[xiv]Op. cit. Charvet. Page 33

[xv]Ibid. Page 33

[xvi]Ibid. Page 34 Note: Shelle Rose Charvet's cited distribution is based on analysis by Rodger Bailey in a document called the *Language and Behaviour Profile*.

[xvii]Ibid. Page 34

[xviii]Ibid. Page 37

[xix]Ibid. Page 49

[xx]Ibid. Page 50

[xxi]Ibid. Page 50 Note: Shelle Rose Charvet's cited distribution is based on analysis by Rodger Bailey in a document called the *Language and Behaviour Profile*.

[xxii]Ibid. Pages 50-52

[xxiii]Ibid. Page 50

[xxiv]Ibid. Pages 50-51

[xxv]Ibid. Page 55

[xxvi]Ibid. Page 55

[xxvii]Ibid. Page 95

[xxviii]Ibid. Page 96

[xxix]Ibid. Page 96 Note: Shelle Rose Charvet's cited distribution is based on analysis by Rodger Bailey in a document called the *Language and Behaviour Profile*.

[xxx]Op. cit. Sobel and Panas. Page 189

[xxxi]Ibid. Page 189

PROPOSALS AND OTHER COMPLEX SALES SETTINGS

This chapter augments Chapter 9's discussion of sales processes for larger-organization proposals and more complex sales settings, and reemphasizes the importance of Best Buyer instruction-centered discussions and select other attributes to heighten your success.

Proposals and Their Challenges

Chapter 6 highlights having a relentless focus on a targeted group of Best Buyer prospects. Best Buyer prospects are potential clientele who have attributes similar to the top echelon of essential clients your firm is currently serving well. These prospects have the complexity, capability, and need to utilize a meaningful level of your firm's offerings. As discussed, when using the instruction-centered marketing and meeting processes discussed in Chapters 7 through 9, you may avoid competitive proposals. That is obviously ideal. Unfortunately, we don't live in such a utopian business world. So, let's make the effort to get great at proposals.

Many years ago, during my partner years at KPMG in Peoria, Illinois, I remember being involved in select competitive proposals. Prospects would invite some of the major firms in the area, including Price Waterhouse, McGladrey and Clifton

Gunderson, among others. The local Price Waterhouse office had an 800-pound gorilla client in Caterpillar Inc., along with other prominent businesses. Occasionally, my KPMG teammates and I would hear prospects whine that PW responded back to their proposal request with a thanks-but-no-thanks letter. Our natural view was that their office was just Cat-focused—I now perceive there was a lot more going on there. With the wisdom of age, I believe perhaps PW's stance was consciously chosen to sidestep costly, time-sucking beauty pageants in which they had little chance to differentiate themselves, and consequently win. It's a lesson from which many of us could model aspects.

It's inevitable that you're going to be involved in challenging proposal circumstances. What truly *is* problematic are situations where the prospective client provides limited access to its personnel, or where they are operating a so-called blind proposal. As Jeff Thull explains in his book, *Exceptional Selling—How the Best Connect and Sell in High Stakes Sales*, "Customers who hesitate to work with you should be carefully scrutinized. If a customer refuses to work within a sensible and high-quality approach, you probably will not be able to differentiate your solutions from the rest of your competition and you are likely entering into a no-win situation. In fact, when prospective clients are unwilling to answer questions, they are usually telling you something very important. They may not be ready to take a serious look at their problems, or, if they are serious, they may well be working closely with one of the other service providers, and are looking for ammunition to support their choice."[i]

In addition, the limited access or blind proposal process:

- Commoditizes your service, so that price is often the main differentiator.

- Introduces additional engagement risk to your firm, since you are not able to adequately assess the environment and personnel at the prospect.

- Creates potential for scope-creep and poor billing realization because the prospect's promises and other representations may not be truly forthcoming.

- Places predominate power of the engagement in the prospect's hands, versus creating a healthy, interdependent relationship.

- Establishes a cloudy precedent for future business dealings with this prospect.

I'm not naïve enough to suggest that you simply walk away from all proposals of the type noted above. In some industries, like colleges, healthcare, governmental, and select commercial arenas, they are common. Notwithstanding limitations placed upon your team and you, there may be ways to access individuals at the prospect, and obviously you'll want to avail any of those chances. Nevertheless, there are times, like those cattle-call proposals involving a huge number of firms, when it may make total sense for you and your team to say, "Thanks, but no thanks," as my CPA neighbors at Price Waterhouse Peoria would do periodically.

Assuming that you've cleared your internal hurdle on deciding to propose, let's examine . . .

Today's Buyer Proposal Psychology

Since the Great Recession, some have observed that there have been changes in the buying behaviors in B-to-B sales transactions. Specifically, authors Matthew Dixon and Brent Adamson, in their book, *The Challenger Sale—Taking Control of the Customer Conversation*, note, "The need for consensus across customer stakeholders has gone way up. Senior decision makers are no longer willing to go out on a limb for any service provider or solution, unless it has the support of his or her team. You've got to build a network of advocacy along the way, or risk losing the engagement altogether due to weak support across the organization."[ii]

Similarly, large-company sales consultants Tom Searcy and Barbara Weaver Smith in their book, *Whale Hunting—How to Land Big Sales and Transform Your Company*, observe, "Big companies . . . have a team of buyers. They want to spread out the risk and responsibility of buying and be certain that all areas that might be affected by a change in vendor . . . have been consulted."[iii]

Searcy and Weaver Smith also observe that, the tendency for larger companies, "Is to seek safety over benefits. For that reason, fear trumps all other emotions in the process of making a decision."[iv]

In addition to the above-noted reliance on buying teams since the Great Recession, research on buying patterns and buyer loyalty articulates that:

- 38 percent of buyer loyalty and attraction is based on the seller/provider's brand, product or service delivery reputation.

- 9 percent is attributed to the provider's ability to outperform on price-to-value ratios.

- 53 percent relates to the *provider's capability/capacity to excel on the sales experience itself*, versus competing firms.[v]

Essentially, buyers are often noting that they're not seeing significant differences in providers capability-wise versus the degree of differences the providers are perceiving among themselves. The meaningful differentiators occur with the *how— the approaches used to influence and sell*. Authors Dixon and

Adamson state that the most critical components buyers note as being differentiators in the sales experience are:

- Offering unique and valuable perspectives on the market.

- Helping navigate alternatives.

- Providing ongoing advice or consultation.

- Assisting their team in avoiding potential land mines.

- Educating their professionals and others at their companies on new issues and outcomes.

Within B-to-B environments, from a prospective client's standpoint, most service providers are deemed already to be capable and have great service, or they wouldn't be at the table, period. The value of the service provider's insights—the new ideas to help that prospective client make money, save time and reduce risk drove the decision to select a particular provider.[vi]

In a separate set of post-Great Recession studies by Mike Schultz and John Doerr, published in their book, *Insight Selling—Surprise Research on What Sales Winners Do Differently*, the authors document that winning providers sell in a radically different way than second-place finishers. Factors buyers listed as being what most separated the winning provider from their second-place finisher were the following:

- "Educated me with new ideas or perspectives.

- Collaborated with me.

- Persuaded our firm that we would achieve results.

- Listened to me.

- Helped our team avoid potential pitfalls.

- Crafted a compelling solution.

- Depicted the purchasing process accurately.

- Connected with our professionals and me personally.

- Overall value from the company is superior to other options."[vii]

Of note, most of the preceding criteria were rated as being vastly different (i.e., better) between the winner and second-place proposal provider.

Based on the above conversation, hopefully the importance of personal attributes like rapport, quality questions, listening, social influence skills, and your mastery of clarifying language patterns—along with the value of your firm availing instruction-centered marketing techniques, resonates even more with you now.

The Best Buyer's Team and Your Approach

As described above, in many proposal settings, you are dealing with a team of individuals from the Best Buyer's company. The team's purpose involves ameliorating risk from the executive level's standpoint, which basically means they may *not* be willing to go out on a limb for you. Further, it requires fostering consensus or agreement among other constituents who are affected by the choice being made.

When you're involved with a team buying proposal, the keys for your success include:

- Identifying the broad Best Buyer Team decision-making roles at play.

- Ascertaining specific individuals from the Best Buyer participating in such roles.

- Matching-up your firm's professionals to applicable Best Buyer decision-making groups.

- Applying appropriate aspects of the I^5—Close Approach with each group.

Let's dig into each phase below.

Identifying Best Buyer Team decision-making roles at play.
Within Best Buyer Teams, there are often dynamic roles interacting to arrive at a decision. We'll refer to these groups as the Deciders, the Effected, Vetoes and Collaborators. Many proposals also have a Pretender, someone having an agenda against you or your firm—or who are averse to making any change in the provider, period. You'll want to sketch-out these folks for each proposal. Following is a greater explanation of each role:

Deciders

As the name implies, the Deciders, act as the party who gives final approval to transact with your firm and you. There is always only one person or set of people playing this role in any sales setting. The Deciders can say "yes" when everybody else on the Best Buyer Team has said "no," as well as quash a proposal that everyone else has approved.[viii]

Obviously, the Deciders vary based on the complexity of each organization. However, at most professionalized companies and organizations, they include the audit committee, board and CEO. How far-up an organization's food-chain a buying decision extends depends on factors such as, the dollar amount of the outlay (and anticipated "price performance"), business conditions at the Best Buyer, the company's experience with your firm/you—along with the expected impact on the Best Buyer.[ix]

The Effected

The role of the Effected, is to make judgments about your product or service on *their* job performance. They will either be directly impacted, or they may supervise those that are impacted by your firm—and consequently their personal success is inextricably linked to the success of the proposed solutions or your firm's performance.[x]

There are usually several individuals in the Effected class with respect to accounting-related proposals, including the CFO, controllers, accounting managers and staff, internal audit, IT personnel and an organization's tax department. In specialized industries, the Effected can conceivably expand to individuals impacting how transactions are measured or enter into an accounting system (e.g., actuaries in insurance, or potentially loan officers at a bank).

Since organizations are looking for broader support on key proposal decisions, interacting deeply within the Effected can be a great strategy . . . as they have the potential to positively sway or adversely derail your opportunity. Avoiding them in your proposal process can obviously alienate such individuals. Satisfactorily answering the question: "How will your firm and your services work for me personally?" is the key means of winning over each of the Effected.[xi]

Vetoes

Vetoes—in contrast to VITOs, or, very important top officers—have as their focus, the firm and the nature of such firm's services, making recommendations based on how well they meet a variety of objective specifications. They cannot give a final "yes," but can give a final "no" to a proposal.[xii]

Furthermore, Vetoes aren't necessarily just at your Best Buyer's place of business. For example, a bank can give the thumbs-down to hiring your firm even though company insiders want you. Your prospect's Vetoes can include a general counsel attorney that disagrees with terms of an engagement letter, an audit committee that won't select your firm on a project for independence reasons, as well as an executive who excludes your firm from further consideration because you don't have a local practice office in their home city. Think of them as a gatekeeper.

Obviously, to the extent you can lessen or eliminate a Vetoes' perceived issues with your firm, that's great. To the extent there are intractable deal-killer issues though, it's better to learn that early in the process and skedaddle.

Collaborators

Collaborators have the special role of guiding you through your sales process by leading you to the above-noted players within the Best Buyer Team, and by giving you information to position yourself effectively within each group. They may be found within the Best Buyer, or outside such organization, such as a strong referral source.[xiii]

Generally, one needs to find and develop this Collaborator's assistance. Collaborators can likewise help you sort through the organizational FOG—the facts, opinions and gossip. Nevertheless, your principal reliance on this role is to gain the best intelligence and direction to help you prevail.

A thought-provoking suggestion for improving the Collaborator's role comes from CEO of Big Hunt Sales, and author, Tom Searcy. Specifically, he advocates using a written agreement with each Collaborator requesting:

- Access to connect with select individuals, including members from the aforementioned Best Buyer roles.

- Priority to assure the proposal process is organizationally supported.

- Mutual communication through the process.

- Assistance with breaking logjams.

- Obtaining clarity concerning cultural issues and other company matters.

See http://www.huntbigsales.com/the-executive-sponsor-agreement/ to examine this one-page document. Mr. Searcy emphasizes that the purpose of the agreement is to assure commitment to the overall proposal process, it is *not* an agreement requiring the prospect to do business with your firm. Recalling Chapter 3's discussion of Consistency and Commitment, and how a written statement can drive compliance, use of such an agreement could be influential keeping the Collaborator in the game.

Pretenders

As discussed above, a Pretender is someone having an agenda—often hidden—against your firm or you, or potentially with respect to making a change, period. The agenda could be due to a variety of factors, including:

- He/she has concern that any change in provider will expose one or more of their weaknesses (and your firm may not be as forgiving as their current CPAs).

- Any change will require more work on his/her part during the transition phase to a new firm.

- Your firm didn't offer him/her a job out of college.

- You terminated his/her spouse, best friend or another relative years ago.

- Fill in the blank _____ .

These individuals may be smiley-faced in meetings, but nail your firm or you to a wall afterwards. An effective means of identifying potential culprits is to ask your Collaborators, as well as yourself, whether anyone will stand to lose if your firm is selected. Your best strategy is to discover any Pretenders early on, and work to defuse their impact on your proposal process.

Ascertain specific individuals from the Best Buyer partaking in such roles. Being cognizant of the various roles in the proposal process is powerful. Working with your Collaborators, start to pencil-in specific names of folks within each Best Buyer Team role. An effective question to ask your Collaborators, and perhaps the Deciders is, "To the extent we are going to agree to work with one another, who would you want to sign off on the decision from your shop . . . and what would you want them to be satisfied with?" Again, capture each name and their presumed role on the Best Buyer Team.

Match-up your firm's professionals to applicable Best Buyer Team members. In the short term, you'll meet and interact with Deciders, the Effected, Vetoes, and any identified Pretenders. Determine which of your firm's advisors match-up with the functions performed by the Best Buyer Team (e.g., individuals at your firm who will be part of your forthcoming prospect visits).

It's critical that your firm's professionals be well-prepared for their upcoming meetings with the Best Buyer Team, and that you thoroughly convey relevant prior discussions with the prospect. Asking redundant questions exhibits poor internal communications at your firm. Shallow questions by your teammates about the prospect's business demonstrates slothfulness. Vague questions about the prospect's industry or that lack incisiveness, can give the Best Buyer pause about your firm's capabilities. In short, the orchestrator of this proposal needs to be satisfied your firm's professionals have their act together prior to convening with the Best Buyer Prospect.

Apply appropriate aspects of the I^5—Close Approach with each group. You and your team are now meeting with members of the Best Buyer Team. Perhaps it's valuable to reemphasize the psyche of buyers involved in more significant proposals and complex sales. As discussed previously, Deciders are interested in creating or developing broad accord in these selections. According to the criteria from *Insight Selling* above, your Best Buyer is seeking your expertise and guidance in making a first-rate choice, as well as wanting a provider who listens and connects. Author, strategist, and CEO of Prime Resource Group, Jeff Thull, in his book *Mastering the Complex Sale—How to Compete When the Stakes are High* notes, "The unifying constants of these sales circumstances are:

- The prospective client isn't fully equipped to make a set of high-quality decisions around the nature of their problem, what to do to solve it, and how implementation should occur to realize full value,

- Multiple decisions are required at multiple levels of the prospect's organization (i.e., there isn't one single 'buying decision'), and

- Because there are multiple decisions, there are invariably multiple decision makers and decision influencers (i.e., there are many organizationally that can impact the choice)."[xiv]

Consequently, your firm's lead professional on such proposal effort needs to be fostering agreement within the Best Buyer's Team as well.

With this in mind, the following are a few specific thoughts about availing the I⁵–Close Approach with specific constituents:

Informing Yourself and Developing Rapport: All of the pre-meeting preparation steps described in Chapter 9 apply for your sessions, whether you're meeting with the Deciders, Effected, Vetoes, Collaborators, or Pretenders group. Know your Best Buyer Prospect and the contemplated attendees as well as possible from your team's research. Build rapport using the methods described in Chapter 2. Your initial questions may vary depending on prior encounters. Nevertheless, you want to be in listening and learning mode.

Issues Are Discovered: During research and early discussions, concerns may have popped-up. Once you've allowed your Best Buyer Prospect to fully answer your preliminary questions (and you've listened and taken notes), you can ask your hosts if they could, repeat any challenges and discuss them in more detail. It's completely appropriate to request that the prospect elaborate on any issues noted, once you've let them fully respond to your initial inquiries. Probe so you fully appreciate the nature and extent of the issues. You likely won't have this type of conversation with many Vetoes, but this step would apply with the other Best Buyer Team groups.

In *Mastering the Complex Sale*, author Jeff Thull highlights the importance of this step. He states, "A very important characteristic of the cast of characters in a complex sale is 'perspective.' In every prospective engagement there are two major perspectives: The problem perspective includes the members of the prospect's organization who can help identify, understand and communicate the details and consequences of the problem. The second perspective, the so-called solution perspective, includes those who can help identify, understand and communicate the appropriate solution."[xv]

By having a healthy cross section of Best Buyer Team members engaging in these discussions, there is a better chance of having the problems and their solutions raised organizationally.

Influence Patterns Are Elicited: In meetings with the Effected, Collaborators, Pretenders, and, especially, the Deciders, it's valuable to elicit both their criteria and direction meta-programs. As discussed in Chapter 9, tee up their criteria by asking what's important to them when working with an advisor. Capture their words precisely! Once they've told you everything that's important to them, probe for clarification. You'll want to listen closely to see if they're making references to how their current provider is dropping the ball on any of the important criteria, because this is where that concern might be mentioned. Their direction meta-programs, which also can be thought of as towards or away-from tendencies, can be teased out by asking why that criteria item is important to them. Note, many influence experts believe that *merely eliciting criteria-related content* can have a favorable, persuasive impact on the prospect.

Intensify the Pain of Their Issues: Recapping what their issue(s) are and how annoying or troubling they can be, or what the costs are in terms of money, time, and risk, might be enough for an initial meeting with the Deciders, Effected, Collaborators, and Pretenders. Be flexible, though, in that it could be useful to underscore these issues with certain prospects—your situational awareness is key. Many CPAs are reluctant to delve into these painful areas. Particularly when it involves throwing another firm under the bus, as it might feel unprofessional. In complex proposals and sales settings, author Thull notes, "The most successful sales professionals recognize that a sale is, first and foremost, the result of a customer making a decision to change. Thus, when they are working with a customer, they are actually helping the client navigate through a decision process, rather than a sales process. A key insight in the large body of psychological and organizational research concerning the dynamics of change is that the decision to change is usually made in response to negative situations, and thus, is driven by negative emotions. People change when they feel dissatisfied, fearful, or at risk in their current situation . . .

"As these professionals approach the sales process from a risk and change perspective, they deal directly, and in real time, with the critical change and risk issues that their customer must resolve. Instead of conveying a rosy future, they focus on helping their customer identify the consequences of staying the same, or not changing their negative present. When they help a prospect understand the risks of staying the same, and quantify the specific financial costs . . . related to staying the same, the decision to buy (which is a decision to change) takes on a compelling urgency."[xvi]

Although intensifying the pain of their issues may not be in your current repertoire, it can *clearly* elevate a Best Buyer Team's action to change. Please review the Chapter 9 approach for activating this process.

Introduce Your FIRM Solutions: To the extent you've anticipated particular issues from your pre-meeting research, and have case studies with you that address their circumstances, it's totally appropriate to unveil or describe how you've approached similar situations in the past. Where one of your firm's professionals has handled circumstances like the prospect's recently, consider scheduling a follow-up meeting with that person, if appropriate. Depending on the significance of their problems discovered in the preceding steps, plan on incorporating FIRM case studies within your proposal document and any oral presentation.

Close: In light of your presumed issuance of a formal proposal, there is less emphasis for what we might normally call a "close." Nevertheless, if an issue has come up that one of your teammates has dealt with (as highlighted in the preceding section), it may make sense to state, "Considering this issue you've been grappling with, I'd like to have _____ from our firm have a complimentary meeting to discuss the matter further with your team and you. Does it make sense to find a mutually convenient time in the next _____ ?"

Post-meeting, if you've promised anything, take care of it pronto—by sending references, scheduling a follow-up call, providing sample reports, and so on. Further, plan on penning a hand-written thank you card to **each** Best Buyer who attended your meeting, no matter their level with the company. It's a nice touch and shows respect for their time.

You and your firm have done a substantial amount of heaving lifting to win this engagement. Now it's time to . . .

Aggregate Findings into Your Proposal/Solution

The process highlighted herein is likely different than the progression used on most other proposals you've been involved with to date. It probably seems far more time consuming than what you've been doing, too. Nevertheless, by taking this structured approach, you'll probably know a *lot* more about your prospective client and their issues compared to other suitors at the table. Of course, when you consider the lifetime value of an essential client, as described in Chapter 6, such extra time investment by you and your firm to land this new Best Buyer will be chump-change.

Proposals are meant to be delivered and discussed in person—you want to be eye-to-eye with your prospect to assess their reaction to items and observe their body language. Depending on the circumstances, it could make sense to describe the proposal as a draft subject to modifications suggested by the prospect in this session.

If you've seen many CPA firms' proposal documents, you'll note they are mostly all about them, including how big they are, why their firm's commitment to integrity and cultural purity is superior to every other CPA firm, how accomplished the engagement team is, how many companies they audit in your industry, and so on. Presumably, if you've been invited to propose, the Best Buyer prospect believes you've got the goods to deliver. Consequently, when the Best Buyer perceives your professionals are pontificating about themselves and the firm, they actually hear, "Blah, blah, blah, blah, blah." Prospects don't give a hoot about you, *they care about their business and themselves.*

What works? As described earlier in this chapter, the biggest differentiators between proposal winners and runners-up include matters such as how you educated them with new ideas or perspectives; how you collaborated with them; how you persuaded them they would achieve the results they're looking for; how you listened to them; how you helped them avoid potential pitfalls; how you crafted a compelling solution; and how you connected with them personally. In other words, *it is their experience with you!*[xvii]

If the foregoing is true, how should you structure your proposal? Conceivably, the proposal should encompass:

- An overview of the Best Buyer Team professionals you met with, which shows you collaborated and connected with them personally.

- Issues discovered, which demonstrates you collaborated/listened to them.

- Consequences or pain of these issues continuing, which suggests your ideas will help avoid pitfalls.

- Subjective areas you observed they want resolved—potentially incorporating the Deciders and Effected members' criteria and direction meta-programs, which highlights listening, collaboration and connection.

- FIRM case study solutions to their problems, which likely educates, persuades the Best Buyer results can be achieved, and represents a compelling outcome.

- Steps you or your firm will take to assure their other key criteria meta-programs will be addressed, which notes collaboration, listening, solutions-orientation, and personal connection.

If you want to talk about your firm for a couple minutes at the end of the meeting, that would be okay.

Such a proposal style would truly be Best Buyer-focused and refreshingly different than most competing CPA firms, wouldn't it?

Of course, select proposals include oral presentations before a board or other group of Deciders. Arranging your discussion utilizing the above-noted methodology makes total sense, too. Although presentation techniques are beyond the scope of this book, there are a number of great reference tools in the marketplace for you to lean on. One of my favorites is *Talk Like TED—The 9 Public-Speaking Secrets of the World's Top Minds* by Carmine Gallo.[xviii]

Chapter 10 References

[i]Thull, Jeff. *Exceptional Selling—How the Best Connect and Win in High Stakes Sales*. John Wiley & Sons, Inc., Hoboken, NJ, 2006. Pages 102-103

[ii]Dixon, Matthew and Adamson, Brent. *The Challenger Sale—Taking Control of the Customer Conversation.* Penguin Group (USA), Inc., New York, NY, 2011. Page 52

[iii]Searcy, Tom and Weaver Smith, Barbara. *Whale Hunting—How to Land Big Sales and Transform Your Company.* John Wiley & Sons, Inc., Hoboken, NJ, 2008. Page 112

[iv]Ibid. Page 117

[v]Op. Cit. Dixon and Adamson. Pages 47-51. Note: the author's conclusions were rooted in a study conducted by the CEB Sales Leadership Council in 2011.

[vi]Ibid. Page 53

[vii]Schultz, Mike and Doerr, John E. *Insight Selling—Surprise Research on What Sales Winners Do Differently.* John Wiley & Sons, Inc., Hoboken, NJ, 2014. Page 9

[viii]Miller, Robert B. and Heiman, Stephen E. (with Tuleja, Tad). *The New Strategic Selling—The Unique Sales System Proven Successful by the World's Best Companies.* Grand Central Publishing/Hachette Book Group, New York, NY, 1998. Page 68

[ix]Ibid. Page 87

[x]Ibid. Page 68

[xi]Ibid. Page 91

[xii]Ibid. Page 68

[xiii]Ibid. Pages 68-69

[xiv]Thull, Jeff. *Mastering the Complex Sale—How to Compete When the Stakes are High*, Second Edition. John Wiley & Sons, Inc., Hoboken, NJ, 2010. Page 26

[xv]Ibid. Page 66

[xvi]Ibid. Pages 72-76

[xvii]See discussion related to note vii above.

[xviii]Gallo, Carmine. *Talk Like TED—The 9 Public-Speaking Secrets of the World's Top Minds.* St. Martin's Press, New York, NY, 2014.

CHAPTER 11

MANAGING THE PROCESS

This chapter focuses on leadership driving behavioral changes via actively managing the growth process at their firm, along with means to accomplish that.

Inspect What You Expect for What's Inspected Gets Respected

As someone that has been in the accounting business for many years, you've surely heard the expressions, "inspect what you expect," and "what's inspected, gets respected." Most CPA firms and their management teams receive gold stars for their scrutiny of production-related metrics at their shops. Your firm no-doubt has a great handle on every professional's chargeable time, and each management member's billing realization, unbilled work-in-process and days-in-receivables. Pretty much everyone knows what they need to do, and that unpleasant consequences occur when results are askew from such expectations. Your CPAs know these metrics will be inspected, consequently, they take meeting them seriously. That imbedded discipline is truly one of the striking facets of the public accounting industry.

At *far* too many CPA firms, operational discipline falls off the wagon when it comes to handling topline growth. Managing topline growth at most shops typically involves reacting well after the fact. Such reaction often means trimming partners or deferring equity partner promotions, versus devising a real strategy to build one's firm, and leading the professionals to achieve that goal. Stoking profitable growth is one of the many hard things CPA firm executives face. But hey, that's why your management team is in the role they're in, and presumably earn the big-bucks, right?

When you think about it, CPA firm production-focused metrics have activities that can be measured in real time and reported on. If someone isn't appropriately chargeable, there are reports reflecting that and available intervention steps, better scheduling or some discussion about what one is doing with their time. If unbilled WIP is excessive, it's conveyed to management and there are likewise measurable action steps to quickly fix the issue.

Contrast those production-related metrics with topline growth. Revenue growth is a result. CPA firm management can obviously measure what that end product is. CEOs and managing partners likewise can instruct their firm's partners to bring in more clients or sell additional services to existing clients. However, those are results too, which are measurable, but are pretty much beyond the real time influence of your leadership team. Sure, they can tell partners their expectations, "We want 12-percent growth, bring in 10 new clients, etc.," but, how can the *actual activities* that drive new fees or clients be swayed?

Notwithstanding the aforementioned limitations, your management clearly needs to craft explicit growth-related goals for the firm. What needs to follow though are contemplated strategies and tactics that presumably will lead to such growth. The *how to*! Following those strategies and tactics are the expected activities partners or managers should execute on to create growth. If the desired inputs to achieve growth are identified— then a firm can create a system to measure and course-correct partner/manger behaviors (related to those inputs) that ultimately influence organic growth.

In the ensuing pages, we'll revisit goals, highlight growth strategies and potential quantifiable tactics—along with accountability and means to capture activities. By excelling at these areas, leadership can inspect what's expected. Consequently, professionals will respect the need to engage in those behaviors that drive such growth.

Growth Goals

Individual mastery of goal setting was emphasized in Chapter 2. Here we will underscore leadership's need for putting a stake in the ground on their firm's growth. As described in Peter Diamandis and Steven Kotler's recent hardback, *Bold—How to Create Wealth, and Impact the World,* "In the late 1960s a University of Toronto psychologist . . . and Maryland psychologist . . . discovered that goal setting constitutes one of the easiest ways to increase motivation and enhance performance. Back then, this was a shocking finding. Shocking because the thinking was that happy employees were motivated employees . . . and that putting too much stress on folks (e.g., by imposing goals) might be bad for business. But they found in dozens of studies, performance jumped by 11-25 percent!" The researchers found that not all goals had the same impact . . . having **big** goals generated the best outcomes (versus incremental, medium or vague goals). Likewise they learned that success came down to attention and persistence—two of the most important predictors to performance. "Big goals focus attention and make individuals more persistent."[i]

Back in Chapter 1, one's beliefs play an important role in persistence. Consequently, firm leadership needs to have a congruent message that the goal is achievable. What are some of the other do's and don'ts? Best practices include:

- Don't establish a goal just because it looks good on paper.

- Communicate the goal frequently, and in a manner that makes it clear.

- Describe the rationale behind the target.

Know that by setting the goal, you're not guaranteeing the result, however, you can expect that the actions necessary to achieve it are going to be pursued relentlessly by all professionals.

With goals articulated, the strategies and tactics to hit them need to be explained and understood.

Strategies and Tactics

Providing a roadmap to your CPA firm's professionals on the *how to* is critical. Many firms and industry teams don't attack the growth process deliberately. They may tell their CPAs to cross-sell $150,000 of business or that they each need to bring in $300,000 of new work, and leave it up to them to figure it out. Certainly, some professionals and industry groups can easily figure it out, but others struggle. Some firms might have 100 different partners using 100 different ad hoc approaches to achieve those objectives. Pulling in clientele from whatever industry. Hum, perhaps firm leadership should hand out "hymnals" so everyone can be singing the same song? Provide some structure to hit the desired target? That's what strategy and tactics do for you. The plans don't have to be overly rigid to work.

For example, using the E^4 Growth Method as a framework, strategies and tactics could be built around components in the following ways:

Essential clients. Essential clientele activities that enhance loyalty and retention might be articulated as follows:

- Identification of each partner's essential clientele.

- Mandate using best practice behaviors, such as in-the-field return preparation.

- Require communication deliverables at the end of major projects that highlight value and suggestions for improvement, such as opportunity letters.

- Conduct post-engagement surveys.

Expansion clients. For these clients with opportunities to deliver additional services, an approach might include:

- Partners or industry team leaders collaborating to identify a set number of clients from each firm professional.

- Via such team effort, identifying and documenting the specific services to introduce.

- Highlighting why such services are of value to the client, and thus should be made available.

- Scheduling meetings with these clients and your appropriate service line professionals.

Emerging issues. With emerging issues, using the approach articulated in Chapter 5 makes sense. Input will likely be needed from your firm's technical leaders and industry directors. Nevertheless the framework needs to include tactics for:

- Educating professionals at your firm.

- Creating tools and client deliverables.

- Identifying clientele impacted.

- Client communications.

- Generating a hook-in-the-system to assure proper billing for the value of the services provided.

Specific guidance to partners needs to be conveyed once the detailed rollout plan is constructed.

External client opportunities. Similar to emerging issues above, your firm needs to articulate your overall strategy towards attracting new external client opportunities. The framework could involve your firm's marketing professionals, industry teams, and outside consultants to construct tactics for:

- Describing what a Best Buyer is, based on your firm's essential clientele profiles.

- Identifying Best Buyers in your marketplace.

- Creating databases and contact information for Best Buyers.

- Crafting appropriate instruction-centered marketing documents.

- Building FIRM case studies.

- Optimizing your marketing approach, such as the frequency of contacts to soften the market.

- Training your professionals.

- Calling to set appointments.

- How prospect meetings are structured.

- Documenting the I^5—Close Approach.

- Restructuring your firm's proposal methodology and documents.

Specific guidance to partners would be provided once the tactics for each of the above are finalized.

Sales management expert Jason Jordan observes that what most leaders are missing in managing and fostering growth are the operating instructions for their professionals. He writes, "Of all the data points we see on our reports, which are the inputs and which are the outputs? Which are the causes and which are the effects? If I want to move this number, should I push this one or pull another? To have control over something, it is fundamental to have an understanding of the cause-effect relationship between the actions taken and the outcome we expect."[ii]

This is why separating a firm's growth goals from the activity expected of their professionals is so critical. Managing certain sales-related activities of your professionals leads to achieving growth goals. The insight is, if you want certain topline growth outcomes, you as a leader must do certain things. Expecting certain growth goals to be achieved without ensuring sales-related strategies and tactics are in place is a disaster waiting. It is a recipe for unpredictable, uncontrollable performance.[iii]

In short, the overall topline growth goal, in and of itself, cannot be managed by your firm or you. However, where you break down those goals into their strategies and tactics, the underlying required activities—no matter if the activities are assigned to partners, marketing professionals or others at your firm—can be tracked and managed by leadership. This process provides the necessary discipline to your CPA firm's growth approach, the same type of discipline that exists for charge-time, realization and the like. Absent such a roadmap, the blind will lead the blind.

Although we'll discuss management-related matters in Chapter 12, my sense is that many firm CEOs and managing partners are exceptional at expressing what goals need to be met. Where they often fall short is in *describing how*. The above-mentioned Jason Jordan, along with sales performance benchmarking firm CSO

Insights, have studied the impact of having processes in place, such as those discussed here. "Their research reveals that those very processes may stoke 23 percent more revenue versus a baseline."[iv] Processes include a variety of other best practices not covered in this book, but specifying goals, strategies and tactics are *the* central components. Monitoring progress and providing accountability are key facets in achieving success too, which leads us into our next section.

Responsibility for Running-the-Play

Accountability and responsibility. Many of us like to hold others accountable and responsible for actions or inactions. We're not as fond of it when others make us answerable though.

In the context of growth management, author Nathan Jamail in his book, *The Sales Leaders Playbook*, views it as foundational to successful topline expansion. As he explains it, "Accountability is the acknowledgement of responsibility for actions, decisions, and policies, and the obligation to report, explain, and be answerable for consequences. The willingness to be held responsible for what you do, and what you fail or refuse to do is critically important."[v]

Certainly, if your firm had no accountability in other areas, like using budgets or inputting time reports, it would be catastrophic. When people are unaccountable, they tend to adopt bad habits, such as procrastinating, approaching work half-heartedly, or finding any multitude of excuses for why an action wasn't taken.

So, if accountability works pretty well in most other operational areas of a CPA firm, why do CEOs and office managing partners shy away from it when it comes to enforcing actions that arguably should generate topline growth? Author Jamail's beliefs are that, leaders at times ignore accountability in the growth arena, because they:

- Don't want to be held accountable themselves,

- Don't want to be perceived as "rocking the boat" excessively,

- Are uncomfortable with or afraid of conflict, and avoid it at all costs,

- Think that spending the time will be too time consuming, and/or

- Aren't exactly sure *how* to hold their professionals accountable.[vi]

If your firm hasn't articulated a sales process until now, and consequently not tracked a professional's activities related to practice expansion previously, having discipline and accountability around expectations will be imperative. It's always more effective to deal with noncompliance when it's new and the issue is small. Remember to inspect what you expect so what's inspected will be respected.

Let's highlight a few points on tracking results.

To CRM or Not

While writing this chapter, I interacted with consulting firms involved with installing software packages at professional service firms, including CRMs. They were *not* supportive of most CPA firms buying a CRM installation, contrary to what I perceived their self-interests would be. Their reasons included:

- Firms haven't discerned what key performance indices (KPIs) drive growth and consequently what KPIs they need or want to track.

- Poor training participation frequently occurs in connection with an installation.

- There is often spotty use of the system by professionals.

- Management doesn't use the data in a timely way from a decision-making perspective.

Essentially, many firms come to them with the idea that a CRM is the panacea to their growth struggles, when there are myriad other issues that require attention first. The CPA firm's leaders are disillusioned when their growth-related headache doesn't subside. Consequently their advice is:

- Determine what KPIs are critical to your growth strategy (these are normally the tactical activities that produce growth).

- Employ a simple reporting process and technology platform, such as capturing as little as four to five data points using a familiar technology tool such as an Excel template.

- Enact a consistent time frame where results must be reported by professionals, such as when time sheets are due.

- Prepare timely report summaries using relevant data.

- Respond quickly when there is either noncompliance with reporting requirements, or activities are inconsistent with management's expectations.

Basically, use familiar tools and a normal reporting date to capture predetermined growth-driving activities. Address nonconformity with the reporting deadline immediately. Obtain summary reports and praise achievers, and counsel those who need it. Treat it just like any other operational metric.

Personally, most of my teams utilized simple Excel-based tools to track growth activity through the years. However, the last business unit I was involved with, a multi-office national practice, implemented Salesforce successfully—which is obviously a far more robust CRM system. No matter what tools you choose to manage topline growth, *consistent use and leadership oversight of the data* are key attributes to achieving structure and driving results.

Chapter 11 References

[i]Diamandis, Peter H. and Kotler, Steven. *Bold—How to Create Wealth, and Impact the World.* Simon & Schuster, New York, NY, 2015. Page 74

[ii]Jordan, Jason; with Vazzana, Michelle. *Cracking the Sales Management Code—The Secrets to Measuring and Managing Sales Performance.* The McGraw-Hill Companies, Whitby, Ontario, Canada, 2012. Pages 7 and 30

[iii]Ibid. Pages 30 and 31

[iv]Ibid. Page 140

[v]Jamail, Nathan. *The Sales Leaders Playbook.* Scooter Publishing, Frisco, TX, 2008. Page 82

[vi]Ibid. Page 82

CHAPTER 12

YOUR EXECUTIVE TEAM—HOW THIS CAN UNRAVEL

There is little doubt that you, as an individual can make *substantial* progress in building your skills by following the principles in this book. Any industry director or office managing partner of a multi-office firm can advance their team's topline meaningfully by availing the E⁴ Growth Method as discussed in Chapter 5 and pursuing the other external client development techniques highlighted in Chapters 6-11. However, to *really* move the needle at your firm, your shop's executive team, and, in all likelihood, board, need to *lead this process*. This chapter might generate heartburn for some readers—particularly CEOs, board members and other higher-ups—so my apologies in advance. Let's start by examining . . .

Carl Icahn's Yardstick: How Does Your Leadership and Board Measure Up?

I was really blessed as a young CPA at KPMG in the early 1980s to cut my teeth on a fair number of M&A transactions. I was a bank-guy back then, and Illinois was one of the hotbed markets for financial institution deals, so there was plenty of action. The 1980s were vibrant days for public company leveraged buyouts too, with guys like Michael Milken and Ivan Boesky often in the news. Another memorable deal titan from the 1980s, a fellow who didn't suffer the same reputational stains that Milken and Boesky underwent, is still working hard at age 79, multi-billionaire Carl Icahn.

Icahn is a self-described activist investor. He notes "Among other things, I'm known to be a reductionist. In my line of work, you must be good at pinpointing what to focus on, that is, the major underlying truths and problems in a situation. I then become obsessive about solving or fixing whatever they may be."[i]

An area that Icahn often pinpoints as problematic involves CEOs and their boards, stating, "Our current system of corporate governance protects mediocre CEOs and boards that are mismanaging companies, and this must be changed."[ii] In a rare public speech, the commencement address at Drexel University in Philadelphia, he articulated the problem as follows:

"One of the major problems in the U.S. is corporate management and the ability to compete. With exceptions, the U.S. has terrible management, and the boards are equally bad. I no longer need *Saturday Night Live* to get a laugh, I just need to show up for board meetings.

"There is a symbiotic relationship between boards and CEOs. As a result, there is no way to hold any of these people accountable today, unless people like me show up and behave as an activist investor. There is no democracy. Investors need to go through contortions to challenge the leadership of companies."[iii]

He goes on to describe how a CEO gets elected, even calling it anti-Darwinian. To explain this, he uses a fraternity president as an example, "Not that all of them are bad people. The point is, he is typically the guy that is always there. Always willing to shoot some pool or have a drink. Comfort you when your girlfriend breaks up with you, or doesn't show up. You wonder when he ever studies, since all the time he's doing other activities. But when it comes time to vote for the fraternity president, he is the one that everyone votes for. This guy then goes into the world of business. A highly likeable guy. Not too bright. Also a good political guy. He doesn't make waves and understands that he shouldn't make waves. He is not a threat to the guy above him. Never has ideas, but is just there. This is how things work today and it is hurting the competitive spirit of many corporations.

"Assume that this guy becomes the CEO. The boards don't care. The first thing the board members do at board meetings is look at their paycheck. The board members typically stay quiet in regards to any explanation that the CEO may give in regards to the bad things that are happening. Then conversation moves onto where dinner will be that night.

"The people running the companies don't know what they are doing. They simply don't know better.

"And this is all a self-feeding, anti-Darwinian problem. The CEO puts someone below him that is slightly dumber than he is. This is simply in order to prevent the CEO from being challenged often, if ever. Someday the CEO steps down and is replaced with the person below him, who repeats the process, putting someone below him that is slightly dumber than he is. By repeating this process, companies might all be run by morons one day. Thankfully, there are exceptions."[iv]

In his closing remarks, Icahn asks that CEOs be innovative, and to go against the trend. "Try something new. Pound your fist on the table. Put your ideas out there, even if it may cost you your job. In the end, have your own imagination and think for yourself! This is what America needs."[v]

I know Mr. Icahn is a little strong—he actually comes across rougher when you watch the YouTube video of the speech because his physiology and vocal inflection are so powerful! I suppose you can be unfiltered when you're worth $23.5 billion. Nevertheless, there are a lot of truths laid bare.

Except for perhaps CBIZ, Inc., practically all accounting and advisory firms are privately-owned by their partners, members, or practitioner-shareholders. My sense is that many of the ills that infect public companies in Mr. Icahn's view, also affect certain CPA firms—with rubber-stamp boards, politically-motivated CEOs and leadership teams, incestuous group think, and insufficient focus on growth, innovation, and excellence. You could probably skim the accounting industry rags for the past few years and make a pretty comprehensive list of those firms.

Unlike Icahn in his activist-shareholder role, certain CPA firm owners *don't* have the luxury to effect change. In fact, speaking up can often lead to retribution. So what's an owner or firm to do?

Leadership's attention and awareness to their relative performance deficiencies can potentially help light a fire to explore options. For example:

- If your firm has been in the bottom quartile of growth in the *Accounting Today Top 100 Firms* analysis over the past three years.[vi]

- To the extent that your firm is continually late to the game with developments, or getting blindsided regularly by competitor innovative services, ideas, and tools.[vii]

- Your idea of per-partner-earnings improvement involves incessantly cutting partners and/or equity partner admissions for worthy candidates.

- You struggle to find outstanding performers to lead offices, industry teams or functional units.

Carl Icahn would likely say it's time for a leadership team wake-up call. Most astute business observers would likely echo that view.

My belief is that most CPA leaders and boards are fairly honest, and ultimately realize when there is a problem. When it finally gets painful enough for your firm and you, set a new standard and step up, or, as Icahn would say, "Try something new, pound your fist on the table, and put your ideas out there."[viii]

Avoid Paying the "Dumb Tax"[ix]

A leadership team's decision to move forward on a practice expansion program is a powerful first step to reversing problematic growth issues. However, *much more is needed to make it happen.* Let's assume your firm embarks on a growth plan or some other change program to improve results at your shop. Let's also assume you've handled potential issues with limiting beliefs and the fears of failure and rejection that can derail the program in its infancy. What can possibly gum-up achieving a favorable outcome? Unforced errors in judgment and execution.

Let's depict what needs to occur to flourish with new initiatives, then highlight common pitfalls that often arise:[x]

Flourishing on New Initiatives

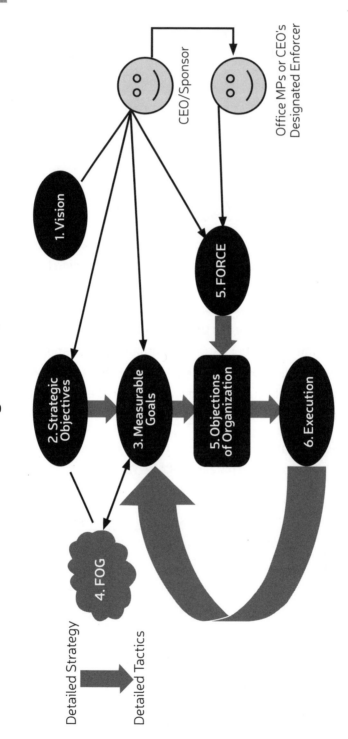

Here is an analysis of the process:

1. The starting point for substantially all successful projects involves the CEO and/or the CEO's designated sponsor (an individual that has received explicit and public CEO support for this endeavor). Such executives paint a picture to the firm of what the immediate challenge or problem is, the repercussions of the existing state continuing on, and what the vision is for resolving the issue.

   Example: If a firm is a bottom-quartile growth firm, and the principal issue the CEO wants to address involves this growth problem, the CEO might describe the situation as follows, *"Our firm currently is in the bottom quartile of Accounting Today's Top 100 Firms in the U.S. in terms of topline growth. The implications for us with this continuing is that we won't have the requisite abundance to create new partners and services, and our market relevance to attract new clients and potentially keep our most important existing clients may wane significantly (since the top-quartile growing peer firms will double our firm's size in the next five years). To counteract these challenges and put us on the path to succeed, we are effecting a new top-line growth strategy that will transform our firm so that we are at least a second-quartile growth firm in the next 18 months, and among the top-quartile growth accounting firms in the next 36 months."*

2. The next essential step involves the CEO or sponsor articulating the overall objectives of this project.

   Example: Continuing the scenario above, the communication might be as follows; *"Our top-line growth transformation will include the following objectives:*

a. *An emphasis on creating raving fan experiences for the essential clients of each office;*

b. *Assuring expansion clients are exposed to the principal add-on services our firm provides for clients in their industry;*

c. *Each office crafting an external prospect plan or target list to attract opportunities with attributes similar to our best clientele;*

d. *Training all management level professionals on state-of-the-art sales approaches; and*

e. *Developing an accountability system for office managing partners and all management professionals."*

3. Once objectives are detailed, goals are built and communicated by the CEO/sponsor.

Example: Following along with the above example, a goals discussion could be as follows; *"Overall, our growth goal for the next year is a minimum 10-percent increase in net fees. This will be achieved by:*

a. *Seeking inflationary fee increases of _____ percent for base compliance fees during the next compliance season;*

b. *Scheduling office managing partner visitations with all upper-tier essential clientele by _____ (date);*

c. *Conducting an independent survey of all essential clients to assess our performance and discern other service-related opportunities;*

d. *With office industry team leaders taking the lead, identifying potential add-on service opportunities for each*

> *expansion client, with the industry leader having oversight*
> *and accountability over partner and manager client follow-*
> *up. The expected net fee increase is _____ percent by*
> *_____(date);*
>
> e. *Office managing partners, along with the office's partners/*
> *managers collectively generating a non-client target list*
> *and contact action plan so that pure organic growth of*
> *_____percent is achievable by _____ (date);*
>
> f. *Beginning immersion sales training by _____ (date),*
> *with 100-percent attendance expected by all partners/*
> *managers; and*
>
> g. *Working with our technology professionals, implement*
> *a _____ (frequency of reporting) system for partners/*
> *managers to update office managing partners on progress*
> *towards growth goals. This system will be effective on or*
> *before _____ ."*

4. The goals and objectives direct creation of applicable strategy and detailed tactics. Strategy and tactics need to be specific, with timelines within the overall goal's parameters. Strategy likewise needs to articulate those responsible for execution, and where possible, how steps can be leveraged to other professionals.[xi]

5. Often when any change project is teed-up, there is inevitably blowback by partners and other professionals, for a variety of reasons. To the extent the CEO, sponsor and other leaders have done an appropriate job on the vision, objectives, goals, strategy, and tactics—it's time to take action. Consequently, the CEO, sponsor or the designated enforcer needs to address the blowback, and assure execution occurs. No excuses, no

explanations. Practical challenges involving tactics may arise, and in select instances tactical modifications may very well be needed, but leadership needs to hold true to the vision, objectives and goals.

6. The results of execution, where strategy is faithfully approached by partners and managers will no doubt provide valuable feedback for adjusting future strategy and tactics. The CEO, sponsor and other firm leaders need to discern valid issues from professionals that have genuinely taken action, as opposed to excuses from those who have not.

It sounds like a pretty simple process, so where do things unravel? Here are some of the more common pitfalls that can generate Dumb Tax:

- No vision is provided by the CEO or sponsor.

- The CEO or sponsor articulates a vision, but fails to follow through on crafting the other critical components listed above (e.g., there are no specified objectives, goals, strategy or tactics).

- The CEO or sponsor fails to stay seriously engaged throughout the entire process.

- The CEO or sponsor delegates a critical role or significant aspect of the plan to an incapable or incompetent person.

- There is a lack of specificity concerning the desired vision, objectives and goals. For example, we're going to grow, as opposed to we are growing our top line by 10 percent.

- Timelines for executing action steps aren't delineated, or adhered to.

- Insufficient training is conducted to build skills, or confidence that the plan is attainable.

- There are little or no consequences for failing to run-the-play.

- There are multiple major initiatives being undertaken by the firm, creating too much noise for professionals.

Excelling at growth plans or other change programs is something virtually all firms have the *capability* of doing. Utilizing discipline to establish the vision, objectives, goals, strategy, and tactics effectively starts the process. The CEO's or sponsor's *resolve* to achieve the outcome, lead the process, communicate repeatedly, enforce compliance, celebrate wins, and otherwise keep the main things the main things will be the ultimate differentiator.

CEO Leadership Profile—John D. Harris

Through my years as a CPA firm partner, I observed, and on several occasions saw up close, the CEO leadership styles and decision-making skills of several firms' leaders. At KPMG, we had two CEOs during my partner tenure, Olive had one throughout, and at BKD three different ones. But for several years my teams and I had more than 100 accounting firms as clients for specialty tax services, and I interacted with, and in many cases got to know well, the CEOs at those shops. With that background, one executive stands out as being able to receive the Carl Icahn seal of approval, John D. Harris, the Olive, LLP CEO from the early 1990s until Olive merged with BKD, LLP in 2001.

Working with John was a real treat, he was, and is, extremely bright—having won the Gold Medal on the CPA Exam in Indiana. Likewise, John had no problem reaching decisions quickly, which is an excellent leadership trait—and changed his mind slowly, if ever, on issues. He also had street smarts, in that he could detect a line of malarkey from a mile away, and had no problem calling you on it.

John also saw the need to adjust and adapt Olive's way of doing business throughout the 1990s, in what was a dynamically changing accounting and business world. For example, he conducted periodic multi-year strategic planning sessions that looked at the state of the CPA industry, developments within the U.S. business landscape, like globalization, as well as technological changes occurring pretty much everywhere, as a framework to set a course for the future, and stoke progress within the firm. Once the strategic plan was set, the firm executed, and John wasn't going to accept poor attitudes or unenthusiastic office managing partners or industry leaders in carrying out the strategy.

Two aspects of our relationship that I *truly* valued was his unwavering support of certain tax initiatives that we executed (one resulted in changing billing relationships/client service responsibilities in most Olive offices to better engage tax partners), and his flexibility to allow me to invest time in start-up niche practice initiatives and crafting tax planning strategies. The seven years that I worked for John was an amazing period of personal growth.

Was John always right, and did we always succeed? No, of course not, it's pretty tough for *any* person or team to go undefeated. Nevertheless, because John had no problem in trying something new, pounding his fist on the table, having an imagination and thinking, our firm made great strides forward, and he made a huge impression on younger partners like me!

Unanimous Agreement Isn't Required—You Just Need a Landslide

An unusual phenomenon I've observed with many CEOs and leaders is a desire to have pretty much *everyone* agree with a plan or proposal before moving forward with it. Some executives almost seem intimidated that they might have more than a handful of dissenters to their ideas. No doubt, it's smart to get plenty of feedback from professionals and others that might be affected by a new strategy or other change in conducting business. That surely helps illuminate otherwise blind alleys for an executive team, and can help tailor the strategy for the good. And, it would be terrific if everybody would then be onboard with your proposals. Unfortunately, unanimous, or near unanimous agreement on any change-related project is just about impossible to achieve.

Trying to adapt a strategic approach or a solution that satisfies every partner in your firm, or for that matter everyone on your board is likely going to water-down the idea so deeply that, even if you were to be wildly successful, the prize would be considerably muted.

An insightful discussion about disapproval-approval comes from Dr. Wayne W. Dyer's 1976 bestseller, *Your Erroneous Zones*, as it relates to reactions from others. Dyer notes, "To put it succinctly, you can never please everyone. In fact, if you please 50 percent of the people, you're doing quite well. This is no secret. You know that at least half of the people in your world are going to disagree with at least half the things you say (and you need only look at landslide elections to see that 44 percent of the population still voted against the winner)."[xii] Dyer continues, "Armed with this knowledge, you can start to look at disapproval in a whole new light."[xiii]

Educated and honest people can genuinely disagree on issues. Your role in leading a growth plan or any change program is to devise the best strategy possible and then, go for it. Getting the perspective of contrary views is absolutely necessary, and can and will make the plan stronger. Be mindful though that people are not going to fully agree with you no matter what. Strive to have a landslide of agreement for your strategy—that is a must—and get started.

Chapter 12 References

[i]Icahn, Carl, August 12, 2014, *The Bottom Line*, Tumblr.

[ii]Ibid.

[iii]Icahn, Carl, June 14, 2008, Drexel University LeBow College of Business Commencement Address.

[iv]Ibid.

[v]Ibid.

[vi]*Accounting Today Magazine* is a publication of SourceMedia. *The Accounting Today Top 100* constitutes intellectual property of *Accounting Today Magazine*. Recalculating the *Top 100* rankings on a three-year basis (and adjusting for major mergers where published data was available) reflects an average per year growth rate, median per year growth amount, and average per year growth rate range of "bottom quartile firms" of .55 percent, 1.5 percent, and -6.45percent to 3.42 percent, respectively. Similarly calculated three-year amounts for "top quartile firms" were 14.31 percent, 13.41 percent, and 11.11 percent to 19.31 percent, respectively. The three-year average per year growth rate for Big Four firms was 10.83 percent—implying healthy growth is possible notwithstanding a firm's substantial size. The three-year period ended with the 2014 data published by *Accounting Today Magazine*.

[vii]See *Strategy—New Practices & Lagging Existing Units* section of www.CPAGrowthPartners.com and Cody, Tamika, November 13, 2013, *Crowe Horwath Appoints its First Chief Innovation Officer*, *Accounting Today Magazine*, for a discussion of one leading firm's focus on growth through product/service innovation.

[viii]Ibid. Icahn, Carl. Drexel University Commencement Address.

[ix]Dumb Tax represents the unnecessary and punitive financial costs—along with leadership's political capital depletion arising from unforced errors in judgment and execution by a company and its executive team. It is a term I attribute to Keith Cunningham, Founder of Keys to the Vault, Austin, Texas.

[x]My former teammate, Steve Martin, a truly gifted professional that has lead multiple successful business-related change projects in this 30-year career inspired this chart's content.

[xi]Creating detailed strategy and tactics are best formulated with a small subgroup

of the leadership team and other interested parties. The framework can be constructed in a relatively short amount of time, using the best information available. Since this is a map, some flexibility is needed to make modifications during execution.

[xii]Dyer, Dr. Wayne W. *Your Erroneous Zones*. HarperCollins Publishers, New York, NY, 1991. Page 63

[xiii]Ibid.

EPILOGUE

Thank you for taking the time to read my book. Making it to this epilogue shows you're a serious student of growth, and I hope you've found answers within these pages to spur topline development at your firm.

Certainly, it's challenging to write a manuscript that appeals to everyone. We are all at different stages of our careers. However, as someone that has built multiple practices from scratch, and successfully marketed and sold services throughout the U.S., the elements and approaches highlighted herein worked exceedingly well. They likewise were the principles I taught to my teammates, and stressed that they needed to master. For the most part, these were skills many other CPAs in the marketplace *woefully* lacked.

So what's *really* important? The answer varies based on your firm role. Following are my perceptions.

First, no matter where you're at organizationally, periodically examining your beliefs is truly important. I've observed young CPAs to high-level executives handcuff themselves—and in the case of leadership, handicap their firms—with limited beliefs. As discussed in Chapter 1, disempowering beliefs are killers, they will keep you on the sidelines, preventing you from making any effort at progress.

A close second in importance involves overcoming the fears of failure and rejection. They, too, act as jailers, often permeating a firm from top to bottom. They are part of the reason you'll see the massive difference in top-quartile-growth CPA firms' expansion rates, versus those shops pulling up the rear of annual rankings.

As an individual, you'll want to focus on the characteristics overviewed in Chapter 2. Since developing rapport is the forerunner to being influential, you'll want to practice the various rapport-building techniques in business and social settings. Similarly, appreciating the need for asking quality questions and listening will serve you well. Finally, having goals and a mechanism to review them, such as availing a goal map like the one pictured in Chapter 2, will potentially keep you on track.

Personally you'll want to be highly attentive to both social proof and liking as societal psychology influencers. As stressed in Chapter 3, having an inventory of FIRM case studies can be excellent tools to convince prospects of your capability via social proof. Further, for good or bad, others *do* judge you based on your appearance, a facet of liking. Although it may seem shallow, adorning yourself in a manner that doesn't detract—but adds to your professional credibility is key.

Finally, comprehending how to set meetings as discussed in Chapter 8, along with understanding the process of conducting initial prospect sessions within Chapter 9's purview, will be critical to getting in front of potential clientele and making a favorable first impression.

Industry, niche practice leaders and office managing partners seeking to grow their units will want to study Chapters 4-7 and 10. Having common agreement of your marketplace differentiators and why they matter, will distinguish your market posture versus competitors. Availing the E^4 Growth Method as noted in Chapter 5, will enable a team to utilize the divergent talents of their firm to stoke growth. Adopting a new client acquisition strategy highly-focused on Best Buyers, those prospects in the market that resemble your firm's top echelon essential clients—and that have the complexity, capacity and need to use a greater amount of your services, can have a significant topline impact. Utilizing an instruction-centered marketing methodology, as highlighted in Chapter 7 frequently can cut through the clutter to gain a prospect's attention, while knowing how to structure your proposal team for complex sales settings, as described in Chapter 10, will help you cover all the bases in these high-profile opportunities.

Firm leaders are in a special role and responsibility level. Consequently, they are in the driver's seat to establish means to manage the growth process in a real-time fashion, the subject of Chapter 11. Further, a leadership team sets the sail of the boat on key initiatives. Chapter 12 addresses some of the common reasons why so many firms fail to advance in the growth arena. No doubt today's accounting firm CEOs wear a lot of hats—and in smaller firms they may have significant client obligations too. Nevertheless, if a firm is struggling to grow, the leadership team needs to take charge.

So, what's *really* important? It's **all** *really* important! Your firm role dictates where your attention should be fixated though.

In conclusion, I love the CPA industry's professionals—and am passionate about seeing your firm and you enjoying even more success now. Further, I strongly believe accounting firms and the professionals at such firms can dramatically change the trajectory of their results, for the good, with effective education, strategy, execution, and perseverance! It doesn't matter how many years you have left in your CPA career, your dedication to mastering the principles from this book will make a significant difference in the years to come!

Best wishes!

Patrick Malayter, CPA, Founder
CPA Growth Partners

APPENDIX A

XYZ, LLP — Client Tax Project/Reference Permission Form

Internal Revenue Code Section 7216 generally prohibits any person who is engaged in the business of preparing U.S. income tax returns from using information furnished to that individual for the preparation of any such return. U.S. Treasury Regulation Section 301.7216-3(a)(1) provides that such tax return information can be used if written consent of the taxpayer is obtained.

This document is intended to provide written consent to use your tax return information for purposes other than the preparation and filing of your tax return. Following is the tax information we wish to disclose (and the format desired):

INSERT DETAILS OF THE TAX PROJECT HERE

Name of Tax Return Preparer/Tax Advisor: XYZ, LLP ("we" / "us").

Name of Taxpayer(s): _____. ("you").

Statements required by Revenue Procedure 2013-14:

Federal law requires this consent form be provided to you. Unless authorized by law, we cannot use your tax return information for purposes other than the preparation and filing of your tax return without your consent.

You are not required to complete this form to engage our tax return preparation services. If we obtain your signature on this form by conditioning our tax return preparation services on your consent; your consent will not be valid. Your consent is valid for the amount of time that you specify below.

I, _____, authorize XYZ, LLP to use, for the purpose of general promotion/marketing, the tax information data highlighted above, in substantially the same format, for a period of __ months from the date of this agreement, or unless otherwise terminated in writing prior to such time by either party to this agreement herein.

If you believe your tax return information has been disclosed or used improperly in a manner unauthorized by law or without your permission, you may contact the Treasury Inspector General for Tax Administration (TIGTA) by telephone at 1-800-366-4484, or by email at complaints@tigta.treas.gov.

_____   _____

[Taxpayer(s) signature]   [Date]

CPA*GROWTH*
P A R T N E R S

DOCUMENTING THE I⁵—CLOSE APPROACH BEST BUYER MARKETING AND SALES PROCESSES

Best Buyer Background Data

Company name _____

Address _____

City/state/zip _____

Contact phone_____

Website URL _____

Business description _____

Other Key Business Information

Fiscal year _____ Estimated revenue _____

Employee #_____ Locations _____

Principal products _____

Principal services _____

Main competitors _____

Service providers * _____

List similar clients_____

Potential influencers outside this company _____

_____

CEO_____ CFO _____

Other executives of note _____

_____

Describe the attributes that make this company a Best Buyer prospect for our firm:

_____

_____

* Service providers currently engaged in audit, tax and/or advisory-related services.

Informing Yourself and Creating Rapport

Describe pre-meeting documents analyzed and any potential issues revealed (reference documents):

_____
_____
_____
_____
_____
_____
_____
_____
_____
_____
_____
_____

Highlight initial questions and areas you'd like to discover more about:
Example: Obviously, our team and I have spent a fair amount of time reading about your firm and you. However, what you read and what happens in real life can differ. I'd love to hear a little about the company and yourself from your perspective. List other potential questions:

_____
_____
_____
_____
_____
_____
_____
_____

Issues Discovered

Document the nature of predominant issues raised by the Best Buyer prospect in your meeting:

_____
_____
_____
_____
_____
_____
_____
_____
_____
_____
_____
_____
_____

Potential questions to reveal the type and extent of issues:
- I'm wondering if we could go back to the point you raised a few minutes ago concerning _____. Could you please tell me more about it?
- It seems like you've got a lot of things going on! I'm curious, are there any aspects of your work-related activities that you'd love to delve into more, or alternately, spend less time on?
- Depending on the answer to the preceding query, you can pose the follow-up question, "What prevents you from being able to do that?"
- You mentioned _____ (their specific problem) as being an issue for you. Is this a petty annoyance or something that needs to get fixed soon?
- Earlier you noted you've worked with _____ CPAs for several years. Presumably all's been well, but, I'm wondering if you had a magic wand and could improve anything about your experience with XYZ, what would that be? Remember, to the extent they say something useful, ask, "Could you please tell me more about that?"
- What's missing in your relationship with _____ CPAs?
- You indicated _____ has been a continuing issue. How much is this costing you (alternately, how much has this cost you up till now)?
- Is this problem with _____ impacting others in your department (alternately, are other aspects of your business being adversely affected by _____)?

Influence Patterns Elicited

Elicit criteria of decision makers:

Example: Obviously, you've worked with other advisors (or whomever their CPA is), up till now. I'm curious, when you work with professionals like us, what's important to you from a client standpoint? Note: Capture exact criteria items. List anything that clarifies their criteria below:

_____
_____
_____
_____
_____
_____

Elicit the direction meta-program:

A good way of pick-out a direction meta-program is by simply listening. Do they discuss items that they want to gain, achieve, get or have . . . or do they describe situations to be avoided, etc.? You can also tease out the direction meta-program by asking questions related to the criteria elicited in the previous section, such as:
- Why is having that (criteria item) important to you?
- What will having _____ do for you?
- What's important about _____?

List your assessment of their direction tendency and any specific examples provided:

_____

_____

_____

Elicit the source meta-program:

The source meta-program concentrates on whether a person is influenced more by external sources, such as feedback from bosses, customers, co-workers, and the like, or from their own internal standards or beliefs, such as, they just knew the client was happy, they did a good job, this was the right decision, and so on. A common elicitation question is, "Who do you involve in the process, when you make a decision about _____?"

List your assessment of their source tendencies and why:

_____

_____

Intensify the Pain of Their Issues

Based on the issues identified, what are the potential consequences to the Best Buyer prospect in terms of money, time and/or risk to the extent these issues are not satisfactorily resolved?

_____

_____

_____

_____

_____

_____

What questions can you ask that would associate the Best Buyer prospect to the pain of these issues?

Example: You've stated how the XYZ accounting firm regularly misses your agreed-upon deadlines. What's that going to cost you when you break your lender's covenants for submitting the audited financials late? Now list yours:

_____

_____

_____

_____

_____

_____

Introduce Your FIRM Solutions and Case Studies

Detail potential FIRM solutions and case studies that highlight how your firm has resolved substantially similar matters, along with any specific client references you could provide:

_____
_____
_____
_____
_____
_____

Close

What are the potential next steps to advance this opportunity?
Depending on the context of your meeting, the close might be:

- Setting up a follow-up meeting with one of your firm's experts where you've identified a painful issue. In other words, where you've found some wedge-issue.
- Providing some complimentary service such as a tax physical or SALT nexus review.
- Proposing on a specific niche project, or a key segment of the relationship.

Identify your possible next steps:

_____
_____
_____
_____
_____
_____

Follow-up Matters

Articulate follow-up steps to advance this opportunity:

_____
_____
_____
_____
_____
_____

Note: this is a general format of the process. For larger proposals and complex sales settings, identification of the applicable parties involved—the Deciders, the Effected, Vetoes, Collaborators and Pretenders—and their issues, will be necessary.

ABOUT THE AUTHOR

Mr. Malayter is a CPA and Founder of CPA Growth Partners, Inc. Prior to launching the Company, he was actively engaged in the public accounting arena for over 35 years as a partner with KPMG, LLP, Olive, LLP—and finally BKD, LLP. During such timeframe, Patrick served as the National Tax Director for both Olive, LLP and BKD, LLP where his teams crafted multiple growth-inducing tax solutions—and where during the Olive, LLP years, the unit was recognized as one of the fastest-growing middle-market tax practices in the U.S. Mr. Malayter likewise founded, or contributed significantly to, the development of six specialty consulting and tax practices which generated multi-million dollar revenues and profits.

Mr. Malayter is distinguished in the domains of people development and training—having served as an instructor for the AICPA National Tax Conference, AICPA National Tax Education Program, AICPA National Construction Conference, Bank Tax Institute—and KPMG Executive Education and National Professional Development programs. He has authored and taught courses involving goal setting and attainment in the professional services world—*Seizing the Reins of Change,* and personal influence/persuasion—*Unstoppable Influence.*

Patrick has a B.S. Degree in Accounting with Distinction from the Kelley School of Business at Indiana University, Bloomington. He has also attained Master Practitioner status in NLP—a communications-based psychology subfield, and has completed clinical hypnosis certification training as a means to better appreciate influential communication patterns.

You can contact Patrick at Pmalayter@cpagrowthpartners.com

NOTES AND IDEAS TO PURSUE